CAN THE MARKET DELIVER?

FUNDING PUBLIC SERVICE TELEVISION IN THE DIGITAL AGE

CAN THE MARKET DELIVER?

FUNDING PUBLIC SERVICE TELEVISION IN THE DIGITAL AGE

British Library Cataloguing in Publication Data

Can the Market Deliver?: Funding Public Service Television in the Digital Age

A catalogue entry for this book is available from the British Library

ISBN: 0 86196 662 7 (Paperback)

Published by
John Libbey Publishing, Box 276, Eastleigh SO50 5YS, UK
john.libbey@libertysurf.fr; www.johnlibbey.com

Orders (outside US): Book Representation & Distribution Ltd: info@bookreps.com
Orders (US): Independent Publishers Group: frontdesk@ipgbook.com; www.ipgbook.com

Printed in Malaysia by Vivar Printing Sdn Bhd, 48000 Rawang, Selangor Darul Ehsan.

Contents

Foreword

Today we are living through advances in technology as momentous as the invention of radio and television. In almost every case, the technology will transfer power from schedulers and broadcasters to audiences. The proliferation of new digital services has significantly widened the choice available to consumers. The fragmentation of audiences as a result of these trends is posing significant challenges for public service broadcasting (PSB). In order to prosper in the broadcasting market of the future, public service providers will have to work harder to persuade audiences to access their content and build brands across a variety of distribution platforms.

Against this background of change, two interrelated debates are currently underway: Ofcom's review of public service television broadcasting and the Government-led review of the BBC's Royal Charter. These essays are commissioned as a contribution to these public policy debates. The views expressed are those of the authors and not necessarily of the BBC, and indeed there are some with which we disagree. However, the BBC's own thinking, as set out in *Building public value* and elsewhere, has been influenced by many of the arguments put forward.[*]

Some commentators argue that these technological advances mean that the age of public value in broadcasting is over. Instead, they say, we should look forward to an era of private value and individual consumer choice in which a perfect new market in programmes and services will be created by encryption technology and subscription.

Most of the authors challenge this view and argue that the need for public

---

[*]   BBC, *Building public value - Renewing the BBC for a digital world.* BBC, 2004.

intervention and funding will remain strong in the digital age, for democratic as well as economic reasons. The essays start from the basic premise that society has particular expectations of broadcasting which the new and expanding commercial market is unlikely to meet. Each essay explores aspects of the funding and delivery of those public expectations and purposes.

Many of the contributors lay out powerful economic arguments for considering broadcasting as a public resource. 'Public goods' like broadcasting or national defence are not handled well by conventional markets. To be delivered efficiently to those who would benefit from them – which, by definition, is the whole population – they require public intervention. Public funding, based on a universal levy, recognises the public good characteristics of broadcasting and ensures a low price and universal availability.

Dieter Helm highlights the powerful economies of scale and scope generated by new digital technology and the likelihood that the media industry will tend towards concentration in the digital era. Both Helm and Andrew Graham raise doubts about the effectiveness of competition policy to address the structural tendency towards monopoly in broadcasting. They see an important role for public service broadcasters, and the BBC in particular, as acting as a counterweight to monopoly power elsewhere.

Several authors also argue that the market is not equipped to capture the social and cultural value of broadcasting and so will fail to supply the kind and range of programming that society as a whole would ideally want. Even after digital switchover, public funding will be needed to make sure television delivers sufficient positive 'spillover effects' and 'merit good' programming.

Bill Robinson et al's examination of the economic incentives of different forms of funding suggests that certain types of desirable programmes will only be made by publicly-funded broadcasters. Advertiser-funded channels are inevitably skewed towards the preferences of attractive demographic groups, while subscription television tends to focus on those services where price sensitivity is the lowest, for example premium sport events and blockbuster movies. With a few notable exceptions, for example in sport, innovation in technology in the pay-TV world has not kept pace with innovation in content.

Dieter Helm, Andrew Graham and Damian Green argue that the case for PSB should not, however, be restricted to remedying 'market failures'. Broadcasting is intrinsically public in ambition and effect – it can keep us informed about society, enable us to participate in public affairs, and make us aware of other cultures and viewpoints. As such, they argue PSB is central to the realisation of many of our rights, as citizens, in a democratic society.

The public value potential of the digital revolution is enormous. It will usher in new ways for people to take part in civic society, personalised learning tools, new ways of connecting communities, and the opportunity for more localised content. The vital role of public service broadcasting in maintaining existing cultural bindings and creating new ones in a fragmenting society is explored by Damian Green.

This will only happen, however, if the new technologies and services are available and affordable to all. With its unique funding and unique mission, the BBC must be at the forefront of creating a fully digital Britain. In particular, the BBC can play a powerful role in enabling the less affluent and digitally adept to make the most of the new technologies, ensuring no one gets left behind.

The BBC, in conjunction with Human Capital, recently conducted the first ever large-scale attempt to quantify the total value generated by the BBC. Simon Terrington and Caroline Dollar outline the results of this research which demonstrates both substantial public support for the idea of PSB and that audiences value it significantly above the resources currently devoted to it. Over 80 per cent of the population is willing to pay the current level of the licence fee (£121 per year) to continue receiving BBC services and on average people value it at twice that amount.

Gavyn Davies, Bill Robinson et al and Andrew Graham offer different perspectives on this research, but all conclude that the introduction of a subscription system for the BBC would lead to a decline in revenue and a significant loss of national welfare. Moreover, the BBC would become a different kind of broadcaster, in competition for revenue with other subscription funded broadcasters and driven by commercial imperatives rather than public service goals. One of its main sources of public value, its universality, would be lost.

The licence fee is seen by many authors as an effective means of paying for services provided by a BBC which is an independent, universal broadcaster, committed to delivering high quality and distinctive content. The licence fee provides a direct connection between the BBC and the British public, and Dieter Helm argues that it should be regarded as a form of 'club fee'.

A recurrent theme in the essays is how the strength of broadcasting in the UK is the result of the way in which the whole fits together: as the title of Andrew Graham's essay makes clear, 'It's the Ecology, Stupid'. The fact that commercial broadcasters and the BBC compete for audiences, but not revenues, has given them both the means and incentive to invest heavily in high-quality, UK-made programmes. Mark Oliver challenges the view that commercial PSB is in terminal decline, and outlines how its future is intrinsically linked with the funding, scale and scope of the BBC. A key area of consensus among the authors is that the BBC must have sufficient strength to maintain its public service impact and provide a benchmark for quality for the whole broadcasting system.

Many of the contributors recognise the value of strong institutions in PSB provision, particularly those with incentives closely aligned to public purposes. Such institutions have clear advantages over primarily commercial broadcasters, though there will remain a need for scrutiny and oversight. Dieter Helm and Damian Green are clear that the BBC must be prepared for a rigorous assessment of its overall efficiency and effectiveness. It has been suggested elsewhere that competition for public funding, via an Arts Council of the Air model, would lead to greater value for money and add to the quality of PSB programming. Jeremy Mayhew and Luke Bradley-Jones' analysis of the New Zealand system, however, raises serious doubts about the efficacy of moving towards a contractual approach to the funding and delivery of PSB in the UK.

The BBC's vision for its future calls for radical changes in attitude and organisation. The key is public value: the BBC should put the public and the interests of licence payers first when it considers what size and scale it should be and how it should conduct itself going forward. The BBC should also consider the legitimate interests of the rest of the audio-visual sector more carefully than it has in the past. As outlined in *Building public value*, any plans for new BBC services will be subject to a rigorous assessment of their market impact, alongside their contribution to public value.

In spite of a rapidly changing environment, public service broadcasting in the UK still matters. While new technologies make it possible to buy and sell programmes and services, this does not mean that it is desirable to leave broadcasting largely to the market. Through its mass reach and influence at the heart of our daily existence, broadcasting has an unrivalled capacity to enrich people's lives as individuals as well as improve the quality of life in society. It is the recognition of this basic fact which has led us to believe that the public interest is best served by everyone having access to a range of services that deliver quality and ambitious programmes, whatever their age, sex or where they live.

Mark Thompson
BBC Director General[*]

[*]   Particular thanks are also due to James Heath and David Levy for bringing this collection of essays together.

Executive Summary

1. Consumers, Citizens and Members: Public Service Broadcasting and the BBC

Dieter Helm

Dieter Helm examines two markedly different approaches to thinking about the case for public service broadcasting (PSB) and the rationale for the licence fee: the economic analysis of market failure and a citizenship-based paradigm. He concludes that there remains a strong case for intervening to encourage the provision of PSB, and that the licence fee remains an appropriate method of financing the BBC.

- Market failure is only one component of the case for PSB. The concept of citizenship is more than a mere extension of the economic view of PSB; it derives from a different set of political, social and cultural values. Broadcasting plays a core role in the functioning of UK society and access to it is important for the realisation of many of our rights and duties as citizens.

- Market failure does, however, give some considerable insights into specific aspects of PSB. The market failures in broadcasting are pervasive and will not be 'solved' by the coming of the digital era.

- The broadcasting market is likely to remain broadly oligopolistic, due to economies of scale and scope and the cost structure of platforms. Rather than a fragmented market with hosts of new competitors, the digital age may well turn out to be characterised by a small number of dominant vertically integrated players, with significant barriers to entry. Competition policy is unlikely to be sufficient to address this structural tendency towards concentration.

- The BBC can be thought of as an example of what economists term a 'club good', with the licence fee as a membership card. The 'club model' leads to the idea of the BBC Board of Governors as 'trustees', with a closer and more direct relationship to the members or licence fee payers. Despite the clear benefits of the BBC's unique mission and method of finance, there remains the need for external economic regulation in order to ensure the BBC is cost efficient.

- The licence fee is more likely to deliver citizenship benefits than other alternative funding mechanisms, since, by including everyone in the contributions to the average costs, the gap between average and marginal costs will be minimised.

2. The Public Realm in Broadcasting

Damian Green

Damian Green avoids the detailed economic arguments which characterise much of the debate about the future of the BBC. Instead, he focuses on the values of public service broadcasting and on what they can contribute to society, whether they will still hold good in the digital age and whether the BBC will remain the most effective instrument to provide PSB in a fully digital age.

- There are non-economic arguments for seeking to preserve PSB even when spectrum scarcity has disappeared after analogue switch-off. Globalisation involves the dilution of national cultures, and therefore puts at risk the mass expression of a specifically UK culture.

- British culture is changing fast, and has become more variegated, but it is still distinct and valued. Cultural bodies which seek to maintain existing cultural bindings and create new ones will be valuable in the digital age. It is, therefore, appropriate for them to receive public support.

- Public service television does not destroy social capital – the set of informal values which groups of people share and which permits cooperation between them – it enhances it. Democratic societies need forums in which opposing views can be discussed calmly, and the increasing availability of partisan media militates against this.

- The BBC is an existing tool which can serve the purpose of providing PSB in a fully digital environment, and viewers say they are prepared to continue to pay at similar levels to today for it. For the BBC to justify its role at the heart of PSB, it must provide public value, treating its audience as citizens rather than consumers.

- The future BBC will need to provide public service narrowcasting as well as broadcasting. This will need stricter methods of governance. There will also need to be competition for the BBC within the public service sector. The risks of discarding the BBC at this point of the evolution of media technology are much greater than the rewards.

3. The UK's Public Service Broadcasting Ecology

Mark Oliver

Mark Oliver argues that much of the public service provision by the UK's main commercial networks is still sustainable and enforceable in the digital age. In particular, the commitment by ITV1, Channel 4 and Five to high quality and innovative home-grown programming will remain as long as the BBC's funding and scope allows it to encourage 'competition for quality'. Diverting public funds from the BBC to commercially funded broadcasters or a new public broadcaster, while aimed at preserving the overall level and quality of public service broadcasting in the UK is actually much more likely to undermine it. More specifically, the essay highlights the following points:

- The provision of public service programming by commercially funded networks in the UK is intrinsically linked with the funding, scale and scope of the BBC. International evidence suggests that – other things being equal – the greater the level of funding for publicly funded broadcasters, the greater the level of home-grown programme funding on commercial network broadcasters.

- The prospects for ITV1, Channel 4 and Five in the digital age are quite positive with new opportunities to exploit scale and scope and limited likelihood of significant revenue dilution.

- The opportunity costs of the specific public service obligations on commercial network channels in the UK need to be calculated with care. Too simplistic an approach can result in a significant overestimation.

- The public service 'compact' with commercial networks in the UK may still be enforceable in the digital age without recourse to direct funding methods. The opportunity costs may well be exaggerated, the scope for creating privileges underestimated.

- The size and scope of the BBC is likely to play an even more important role in encouraging public service provision on commercial networks in the digital age. The provision of public funding to commercial broadcasters is likely to risk significant 'crowding out' of existing commercial programme investment.

- Any attempts to redirect public funding from the BBC to commercially funded broadcasters are likely to shrink significantly the overall provision of public service programming in the UK. Attempts to split public funding between rival public organisations risks reducing the pressure on the commercial networks to maintain their commitment to high quality and innovative home-grown programming.

4. Measuring the Value Created by the BBC

Simon Terrington & Caroline Dollar

This essay is based on the results of a recent study conducted by the BBC and Human Capital. The study represents the first ever large-scale attempt to quantify the total value that the BBC is perceived to generate. Previous studies have concentrated on what people would be prepared to pay if the BBC became a subscription service. This research looks at both the value the BBC generates for consumers and how much it is worth to society as a whole. This total value includes the value that the BBC creates for citizens through promoting educational development, social cohesion and democratic knowledge. The essay discusses the following key findings from the research:

- There is widespread public support across the UK for the licence fee. 81 per cent of the UK population is willing to pay the current rate of £121 a year and on average people value the BBC at twice that amount.

- The BBC is valued most highly by young people, the better-off and those with digital television. Multi-channel has in some ways set a high benchmark for the cost of the BBC.

- All of the BBC's constituent services are perceived to deliver more value than they cost and the digital services are valued particularly highly. Their low cost-base means they can provide excellent value for money.

- The respondents who place the highest value on the BBC also tend to give the highest approval ratings. Approval ratings are determined mainly by people's perception of programme quality. The most popular programme genres are news, regional news and soaps.

- We estimate that in order to maximise its revenue as a subscription service, the BBC would have to charge a price of £13 per month. As a consequence, only 14.8m households (two thirds of the population) would choose to subscribe and these would tend to be the most affluent, educated members of society. This loss of universality would undermine the BBC's delivery of its public purposes.

- The BBC would lose around £500m a year in revenue, causing a potential downturn in quality. Over and above this, the population as a whole would lose £300 million of consumer welfare every year.

5. 'It's the Ecology, Stupid'

Andrew Graham

Andrew Graham argues that, from the Peacock Report right up to the present, two perspectives have dominated the discussion of broadcasting. One is represented by those who argue that broadcasting should become predominantly a commercial activity; the other view is that broadcasting displays special characteristics and that a substantial role for public service broadcasting is still required if the UK's successful broadcasting ecology is to be preserved. Against this background, the essay highlights the following points:

- The view that digital technology makes the buying and selling of television programmes just like other goods and services is mistaken, because broadcasting continues to be a public good.

- Those who argue that the BBC is currently too large are either ignoring the long run trend in the BBC's audience share and/or they overlook the beneficial effects of a substantial presence for the BBC as a 'standard-setter' and as an enlarger of choice.

- Pro-competitive regulation may not do all that is required, primarily because of the long time lags involved. As a result, the presence of the BBC as a counterweight to concentration elsewhere remains useful.

- Recent evidence shows that, viewed just from the perspective of the *consumer*, the value placed on PSB of £5.4 billion is substantially above Ofcom's estimate of the total cost of PSB at some £3 billion.

- The true value of PSB will be even higher than £5.4 billion because of externalities, merit goods and political rights. One estimate that makes *partial* allowance for these factors suggests a value of over £6 billion. Allowing *fully* for these would put the value higher still. This is because surveys of individuals cannot properly allow for imperfect information and less than complete altruism.

- Ofcom's proposed Public Service Publisher (PSP) is an interesting suggestion. However, *as a stand-alone entity* it is unconvincing as a way of providing extra PSB. It runs the risk of ghettoizing PSB and it is doubtful whether it would be large enough to establish a clear brand. It would be much better to reinforce the UK's existing ecology by ensuring a vibrant BBC and a Channel 4 that is able to provide PSB in competition with the BBC.

- Competition amongst regulators is also healthy so it would be a mistake for Ofcom to be required to regulate the BBC as well as all the rest of broadcasting.

6. Paying for Public Service Television in the Digital Age

Bill Robinson, John Raven and Lit Ping Low

The authors re-examine the argument that funding methods determine the kind of programmes made by broadcasters and that certain kinds of desirable programmes will only be made by public service broadcasters. They find that although there is no reason in principle why subscription-funded broadcasters should not make PSB programmes, recent developments suggest that in practice they do not do so to any significant extent. The BBC, as a commercial subscription service, might well meet PSB objectives, but there would be a clear welfare loss from replacing the licence fee with voluntary subscriptions. More specifically, the analysis arrives at the following conclusions:

- Although broadcasting is now excludable, it is still non-rival, so most of the arguments from welfare economics for the public provision of broadcasting remain intact. The fact that you now *can* charge for broadcasting does not mean that you *should*.

- The case for PSB now rests on the desirability of using public funds to encourage the production of quality television programmes which serve certain public purposes and which the market would not supply.

- Advertising-funded broadcasters have little incentive to make such programmes. They are primarily concerned that programmes are watched, not that they are valued. The past practice of imposing PSB obligations on ITV1 and Channel 4 is threatened by the rapid erosion in the value of those licences in the multi-channel world.

- There are good economic reasons why the market in individual programmes (pay per view) remains small. Bundling programmes into channels and charging by subscription is likely to dominate pay per view as a way of maximising both revenues and welfare.

- This economic efficiency of subscription funding suggests that the BBC could supply PSB programmes as a voluntary subscription service. This would avoid the welfare losses that a compulsory licence fee imposes on those who do not value the output of the BBC.

- However, our analysis of the demand for BBC services, based on research conducted by the BBC and Human Capital, shows that the replacement of the licence fee by subscription would increase the cost to viewers by 30 per cent, reduce revenues (and hence the value of programmes) by 14 per cent, and exclude 10 million viewers.

- The welfare gains from abolishing compulsion are estimated at £300 million, but the welfare losses from the higher licence fee are more than double this figure. This analysis suggests that a compulsory licence fee produces higher social welfare than voluntary subscription.

7. The BBC and Public Value

Gavyn Davies

Gavyn Davies explores what can be learnt from economics to inform the debate on the renewal of the BBC's Charter in 2006, and in particular what economics can contribute to answer the basic question of why the BBC should exist at all. The essay makes the following key arguments:

- Market failure is a necessary condition for the BBC to exist in its present form. It is not a sufficient condition, but those who hope to justify the existence of the BBC on social or cultural terms without placing market failure at the centre of their case face an uphill struggle.

- Despite widespread assertions that market failure in broadcasting is being eliminated by technical change, the market in the new Charter period will continue to under-supply Reithian broadcasting services intended to inform, educate and entertain, relative to the social optimum. Broadcasting will remain a public good in the digital world and those who argue that changes in technology have eliminated the case for the BBC are wrong.

- The licence fee funded BBC creates well over £2 billion of consumer surplus, or national welfare, each year. In order to maintain its ability to contribute this amount to national welfare, the BBC should not be allowed to shrink in relative terms. This is what would happen, notably relative to BSkyB, with a real terms freeze in the licence fee in the new Charter.

- A subscription-based BBC would exclude millions of households, and would generate much less consumer welfare than the current licence fee system. There would be some net gainers, but they would be in a minority, and the nation as a whole would lose. Nevertheless, the needs of the minority – probably concentrated among the ethnic minorities and the lower income groups – are important and should be addressed by re-orienting parts of the BBC's output.

- While the BBC is not the only way of addressing this persistent market failure, alternative models for government intervention and regulation are at best unproven. Ofcom will be severely stretched to prevent the commercial sector from moving towards greater monopoly along with less public service broadcasting. It should focus its attention on this massive task, rather than seeking to extend its power over the BBC.

- Market failure is in some ways much more obvious in broadcasting than it is in health and education, which are not public goods. Other public services like law and order and the road system also exhibit fewer of the characteristics of market failure than Reithian broadcasting. People should remember this before calling for the BBC to be privatised.

8. Contestable Funding: Lessons from New Zealand

Jeremy Mayhew and Luke Bradley-Jones

The authors assess the funding arrangements for public service broadcasting in New Zealand. The scale, source, and means of allocating public funding for PSB directly affect the form and effectiveness of its delivery. One possible approach to PSB funding is a contestable model, whereby public money is allocated from a central fund to broadcasters or producers, via a competitive tendering process, to support specified production activities. This type of model has been in place in New Zealand since 1989 and continues to be the primary means of providing public funding of PSB.

- The primary strengths of the New Zealand contestable model have been: first, it has made PSB funding and delivery more clearly accountable, from a regulatory perspective; and, second, it has promoted competition and plurality in the supply of PSB.

- The primary weakness of the New Zealand funding system has been that it has not effectively and consistently delivered high quality, high impact PSB content. This is in large part because the system is predicated on a non-broadcaster body procuring delivery against a set of cultural and social objectives that are not always easy to define, from a commercially focused broadcast market.

- Contestable funding is effectively a contract-based approach to PSB provision. Because such an approach relies on clear, up-front definition of terms, it has been most successful in securing the delivery of those aspects of PSB which can be specified. New Zealand on Air (NZOA) has been able to deliver increases in hours of local content and of core PSB genres. NZOA has been unable, however, to specify or purchase the 'quality of service' of PSB delivery.

- In light of the lessons from New Zealand, however, it is difficult to imagine that a contractual approach could satisfactorily replace existing institutions in the delivery of PSB. Given the inherent difficulty in defining particular aspects of the prescribed purposes and characteristics of UK PSB, institutions such as the BBC and Channel 4, and the experience, skill sets and ethos they have built up over an extended period of time, seem better equipped to meet the challenge of 'maintaining and strengthening the quality of public service television broadcasting in the United Kingdom'.

• A form of contestable funding could, however, potentially be used to procure some of the elements of PSB provision that may be given up by ITV. In this respect, a contractual approach to the procurement and funding of specific, clearly defined areas of PSB could complement and strengthen the UK's core institutional PSB system.

1

Consumers, Citizens and Members: Public Service Broadcasting and the BBC

Dieter Helm[1]

1. Introduction

The current review of the BBC's Charter provides an opportunity to reconsider the role of the BBC and the provision of public service broadcasting. On previous occasions, the historical context has played a core part in such assessments. The initial development of television, the duopoly model and the creation of Channel 4 and BSkyB all changed the market context, providing new challenges to the BBC and offering the prospect of more pluralistic methods of delivering public service broadcasting.

In this review, the key 'new' issues are the coming of the digital era, and the convergence of telecoms, the Internet, satellite and terrestrial technologies, which offer the prospect of multiple channels and delivery mechanisms, and, with them, a much greater diversity of programming and information sources. The scope for consumer choice is widening significantly, as is the opportunity for producers to access the market. Physical entry barriers are falling.

To some, this cornucopia of new opportunities will usher in a new age in broadcasting and publishing, one in which new forms will emerge, existing ones

1   The author gratefully acknowledges the support and assistance of the BBC in preparing this essay. The views expressed are, however, entirely the author's own.

will have to transform themselves or wither away and new regulatory and institutional approaches will be needed. This new historical context has naturally led many to question: whether the BBC in its current form will be needed at all; whether public service broadcasting should be left largely to the market; whether the market failures will be solved; whether support for particular kinds of programme should be specific to any channel; and, whether the licence fee can be justified.

These questions are complex, and are unlikely to have simplistic answers. Answering them is made more difficult by the plethora of powerful vested interests in the broadcasting market. The BBC naturally wishes to defend the *status quo*, and particularly the licence fee. BSkyB has accumulated market power of its own, through vertical and horizontal integration, and would be a major beneficiary from any dismemberment of the BBC. ITV is sandwiched in the middle, and would face serious competition in the advertising market were the BBC to turn to commercial revenue. Commercial radio might benefit from a BBC forced to rely on the market to pay its way, though it would also face an advertising squeeze. For these reasons, the Charter Review is also the setting for a scramble to lobby for the economic rents which market power brings.

This essay assesses *some* of the main issues: the case for public service broadcasting, the likely operation of the market including the BBC, the financing options and the regulatory framework. In addressing these issues, the recent contributions by Ofcom (2004a and 2004b) will be critically assessed. It will be argued that market failure is only *one* component of the case for public service broadcasting, and it will question the claim that the digital revolution will 'solve' the market failures. It also presents the outline case for the licence fee as a membership fee for public goods, and hence argues a positive case for its retention (in a modified form), rather than as merely the least-worst option.

The scope of the essay is deliberately wide, but it is also a summary rather than a detailed analysis of each of the issues. As noted, the broadcasting market has been subject to decades of academic research, and the BBC's history has been written up in immense detail. There have been numerous reports and commissions. It is not the intention here either to summarise this voluminous literature or to add new empirical research. Rather, the aim is to sort out the arguments and bring them together into a coherent overall policy analysis.

The structure of the essay follows the lines of the argument. Section two discusses the grounds of the debate, and in particular what role economic considerations should play. Section three focuses on the multiple market failures, including market power and public goods. Section four looks at government and regulatory failure, the form of intervention and its impact on independence, and, in this context, the structure and role of the BBC. Section five considers the licence fee and the alternatives. Section six concludes.

2. The grounds of the debate

A starting point in considering the technological context and its implications for the future of public sector broadcasting is Ofcom's contribution to the Charter Review – in particular, its two published papers: *Ofcom Review of Public Service Television Broadcasting: Phase 1 – Is Television Special?* (Ofcom 2004a), and *Ofcom Review of Public Service Television Broadcasting: Phase 2 – Meeting the Digital Challenge* (Ofcom 2004b). Not surprisingly, Ofcom has taken a largely economic view of public service broadcasting, and described it primarily in terms of market failure. This is also the perspective taken by Gavyn Davies, ex-Chairman of the BBC (see Chapter 7). The difference between these contributions is that, for Ofcom, the coming of digital services will 'fundamentally alter the shape of the market' and, by implication, the role of the BBC.[2] This is because Ofcom argues that conventional market failures to provide what consumers are willing to pay for will be much reduced, and in consequence the extent to which there needs to be intervention for *this* reason is reduced accordingly. Davies sees the market failures as enduring – including the mainstream failures in relation to public goods, externalities and information. Indeed, he suggests that the risk of ever greater market power being exercised by BSkyB is an *additional* reason for preserving a licence fee-financed BBC.

In Ofcom's Phase 2 paper, a number of conclusions are drawn. Surprisingly, given Phase 1, Ofcom concurs with Davies that a licence fee-funded BBC is core to the delivery of public service broadcasting, but then goes on to suggest the creation of a new partial competitor as a 'Public Service Publisher' (PSP), challenging both the BBC's main broadcasting output, but also its web-based services. Thus, although the digital technology will usher in much more competition, it will not replace the need for major intervention and the competition will be insufficient, requiring a new competitor to be created as an act of policy.

The Ofcom and Davies approaches are overwhelmingly *economic* in nature, and contrast markedly with political and cultural perspectives. And, whereas the economic approach is largely within a well-defined paradigm, the latter are diffuse and less coherent. The starting point for most is the Reithian conception

2   Ofcom (2004a) p. 8.

of public service broadcasting, which has been overlaid with concepts such as 'values', 'citizenship' and 'democracy'. A decent society requires access to a culturally integrating media.

These are not necessarily mutually exclusive. The objectives of policy intervention are numerous and varied. It is widely acknowledged, including by most economists, that economic efficiency – the basis of the market failure approach – rests upon a very narrow value system. It treats people as rational utility-maximising agents, seeking out least-cost solutions. Human nature, and human values, are much broader, and concern for freedoms (positive and negative), equality and justice are also part of the public interest calculus. To argue that only economic efficiency matters is to rule out much of importance in political and social considerations.[3]

There is then no justification for an economic methodological imperialism in considering the case for public service broadcasting. Although Ofcom, in its first paper, is careful to allow for the concept of citizenship, it is not surprising that a predominantly economics-based regulatory body treats this concept as a form of residual market failure – and, indeed, its concept of citizenship is a narrow one. For Ofcom, the market failure paradigm is *the* perspective from which to analyse the broadcasting market, thereby reducing these plural sources of value to a special case, to be traded off against other market failures. Davies goes further, and sees the problem almost entirely in the economic context. But whilst anything *can* in principle be described as consistent with utility-maximising behaviour, and anything *can* be brought within the market failure framework, it does not follow that interventions *should* be based only on this framework. Markets, it can be argued, exist within a *social* context, with all its politics, freedoms and cultures, rather than the other way around. At stake here is something very fundamental. In discussing public service broadcasting, whilst economics and the market failure framework have a great deal to offer, their universalisation of the problem should not simply be assumed.

'Citizenship' as a central organising concept for these wider political, cultural and social concerns, while somewhat simplistic, has considerable merit, the key characteristics being *equal* status and treatment. Membership of the society is, in the citizen sense, not dependent on initial wealth or income. It accrues to each person *on the same basis*, and this in turn translates into the democratic ideal,

---

3   The literature on non-utility information is a vast and rich one, incorporating much of the discussion in moral philosophy concerning utilitarianism. In the economics literature, Amartya Sen's classic paper on 'Personal Utilities and Public Judgements' provides a core reference (Sen 1979). See also Cohen (1995), Chapter 2, Broome (1999), Chapter 2 and Dasgupta (2001), Chapter 4.

which gives each member of the society an equal say.[4] Much of the welfare state is designed on this principle of equal status: from health and education services, through to the nationwide definition of most entitlements.

Contrast this with the economic model of market failure. Failures on the demand side relate to consumers' ability to gain utility from the spending of their income, and those on the supply side are set in the context of profit- or rent-seeking firms. In the economic marketplace, people are treated *unequally* – what matters is how much they are both willing and *able* to spend. In the democratic political market, ability to pay is not a relevant criterion.

The distinction is not just the well-known issue of income inequality – which can in principle be solved by redistributive social security policies.[5] It has much broader dimensions. These include the provision of goods rather than money, treating the problem not as one in which people need to be empowered to choose, but rather as something that ought to be provided in a particular form, separate from the choices people would make. Citizenship includes rights *from* society – rights to be informed, to be able to vote, and so on – and obligations and duties, many of which cannot be provided unless citizens are informed.

The implications of this distinction between the consumerist and the citizenship concepts of unequal and equal treatment are profound. Citizenship is not just another sort of market failure, it derives from a different set of values. As long as it can be shown that the media plays a core role in the functioning of a society, and access to it is a necessary condition for a well-functioning democratic society, then the level, content and charging basis for public service broadcasting cannot be encapsulated solely in the market failure paradigm. The economists' approach offers one – very important, necessary – facet of the case, but it is not, and could never be, sufficient.

3. Multiple market failures: public goods and monopoly

As a *necessary* part of the case, market failure does however give some considerable insights into specific aspects of public service broadcasting. It cannot dictate the optimal level of provision, or of financing, except in so far as

---

4   David Marquand's *Decline of the Public* makes this point and shows how it conflicts with what he describes as the '*Kulturkampf*' of the economic ideas of the 1980s and 1990s (Marquand 2004). Although he perhaps goes too far in playing down the role and vitality of market forces, the distinction between the public sphere – in which the BBC would undoubtedly be set – and the private is important to the public service broadcasting debate.

5   There is a role for some grading of the licence fee to reflect ability to pay, especially where some marginal viewers might be excluded from enjoying the public good of broadcasting, as we discuss below. However, this is an additional issue, and not a solution to the citizenship problem discussed here.

the efficient solution is sought in the narrow utility-maximising sense. It can, however, suggest the extent to which markets will provide public service broadcasting, and what the outcome might be of a laissez-faire approach.

Perhaps surprisingly, given the extensive literature, there remains considerable confusion about the market failures in broadcasting, and in particular how they influence the design of policy. While pro-market advocates downplay the failures and stress the extent of government failure, interventionists emphasise the opposite. In part, it is an empirical issue, beyond the scope of this essay. But it is also a conceptual muddle too, at the heart of which is the multiple nature of the failures and the public good characteristics of some forms of broadcasting.

Multiple market and regulatory failures

The first – and generally neglected – point to make about market failure is that it is typically *multiple*. Whereas most economic analyses take each market failure in turn for reasons of analytical simplicity, the policy problem is set in the context where these failures happen *simultaneously*, and indeed may reinforce or offset each other. In the broadcasting case, as we shall see, the interactions of market failures tend to exacerbate the inefficiencies of a purely market solution.

The second point is that market failures rarely point straightforwardly to state provision or *single-form solutions*. Markets fail *relatively*, not absolutely, and because the failures are multiple, so the policy instruments tend to be multiple too. Thus, if we see broadcasting as contributing to information, education and entertainment, then we have competition policy, educational budgets, direct arts support, academic funding of research, as well as the financing system for the BBC. Public service broadcasting – in its deep and full form – is not simply created and sustained through the licence fee. The licence fee is one of a whole range of interventions.

Multiple market failures prevail in most markets, though the combinations and interactions differ. In the publishing market, for example, there are many firms competing with each other. But it is not strictly a competitive market in the economic sense, since there are multiple interventions to address a number of market failures, including the public goods and citizenship concerns. Like broadcasting, the publishing market has evolved a complex set of institutions to address these. The production of books, journals and research materials is one that is far from being purely market-driven. Editors, journals and presses are often not-for-profit, backed by grants, subsidies and the support of the universities and their funding bodies, as well as a host of other grant-giving organisations, from the Arts Council to local charities. The publishing world has

6

long since passed through the equivalent of the digital age, with multiple outlets, but interestingly, there is no evidence that the need to intervene, or the actual level of intervention, has gone down. Nor, interestingly too, has new competition led to an obvious decline in market power for the dominant incumbents. On the contrary, in those areas that involve public goods, concentration has arguably gone up.

These considerations set the policy context in a much richer and broader framework than simply public goods and monopoly market failures. As we shall see, the failure of market power in broadcasting is not an isolated one – it is intimately linked to the pervasiveness of public goods, which create the cost conditions that typically benefit size. Similarly, the pervasiveness of branding of bundles of programmes – which is what channels are – derives from economies of scope and scale. It is no accident that BSkyB, the BBC and other core broadcasters tend to be large and vertically integrated, nor, as we shall see, are there good reasons to think that this market concentration is likely to fragment with the coming of the digital age. For fundamental economic reasons, broadcasting tends to be oligopolistic.

Public goods

Normal economic goods – private goods – are supported by property rights, and markets allow these rights to be exchanged between producers and consumers. These property rights have two fundamental characteristics: they are *rival* and *excludable*. By contrast, a public good, in formal economic terms, is *non-rival* and *non-excludable*. It is non-rival because the fact that one person watches a television programme does not impair another's consumption simultaneously. The marginal cost of the additional viewer is zero. Consumers are not rivals, as they are for most economic goods and services. It is non-excludable because there is no obvious way to exclude people from watching a programme, unless some artificial barrier is created – for example, through a law that requires a licence to be bought, or some device giving access to a particular programme. But exclusion needs to be *created*, and hence a property right manufactured.

It is these two fundamental properties which distinguish public goods from private goods: in effect, there are two market failures occurring concurrently. If consumption were rival, but non-excludable, there would be externalities. If excludable, but non-rival, then we would have so-called *club goods*, and as we shall see, the licence fee in effect turns broadcasting into a club activity. Note, too, that there are other externalities in addition to those associated with the public good described here: production and consumption by some individuals affect others in ways that go beyond the fact that the marginal cost of consumption is zero and viewers cannot be excluded. Some of these externalities are part of the public service broadcasting requirements, since a well-functioning society is one where other people are informed and educated, and share common experiences and understanding. So, to complicate matters further, there are multiple externalities as well as the externality in public goods. This is important because 'solving' the public good problem is not sufficient to 'solve' the public service broadcasting problem; it is only necessary.

It is asserted by Ofcom in its Phase 1 report, and by others, that the coming of digital broadcasting largely 'solves' the public good problem in respect of consumer choice for programmes and broadcasting that they are willing to pay for. This is clearly not correct. Nothing in the digital world changes the basic point that the marginal cost is effectively zero. *Excluding people does not make a product rival.* What digital programming may do is to *fragment* the market, and therefore disaggregate the public goods. As a result, the number of people who enjoy the zero marginal cost output is reduced for each programme or channel, and therefore the number of people who might be persuaded – through charging – to contribute towards the fixed costs falls.[6] But since *any* charge will deter at least some consumption at the margin (those people who value the output just above the marginal cost of zero), this can have the perverse effect of raising the average cost to all those paying, hence removing more people at the margin.[7] (Indeed, it is this effect that bites most heavily into the citizen and equality-of-access arguments discussed above under the concept of citizenship.)

In practice, the public good arguments are much wider than the marginal cost of viewing. Programme production involves the creation of ideas, concepts and knowledge, which, once created, has zero marginal cost, and in a well-functioning society may need to be very widely distributed. There is a very large technical literature on intellectual property, R&D and public goods, and the incentive problems to draw upon, and it is notable that all developed countries have significant public support for research and cultural activities.[8]

---

6   There is a parallel with the 'natural monopoly' arguments in the public utilities, where the economic problem is to recover the fixed costs from users or taxpayers, given that the marginal cost is zero, except at congestion points.

7   Myles (1995) Chapter 9 provides a succinct summary of public goods theory and the implications of the Samuelson rule for the optimal provision where the sum of the marginal rates of substitution is made equal to the marginal rate of transformation, thereby gathering together under the demand curve all the consumer surplus that has any positive value.

8   These market failures are well recognised in British policy. See, for example, HM Treasury (2004), for a flavour of the scale of interventions.

The exclusion component of public goods is typically 'solved' in the economics literature by one of three mechanisms: state provision (as, for example, in defence, police, and fire services); by a mix of state and voluntary contributions (for example, coastguards and organised religions); or by the creation of property rights – in particular, the creation of 'clubs'.[9]

Although there are many international examples of direct state provision of broadcasting, these are vulnerable to bias and state propaganda and hence fail the test of *independence*, to which we return below. Voluntary public provision of broadcasting has a long tradition, but tends to be restricted to specific interests rather than public service broadcasting in general, and is liable to capture. Religious broadcasting is perhaps the best example here.

That leaves clubs – a much under-researched approach to public service broadcasting. Club goods, in economics, are those that are non-rival to members: each member pays a membership fee, and then has non-rival access to the service. Since the membership fee is fixed independently of actual consumption, the marginal cost of consumption *for members* is zero. Hence, not only is non-rivalry preserved, but at zero marginal cost. The non-excludability is solved by the criterion of membership, and it requires enforcement. Non-members must not be able to benefit. The membership fee itself recovers the costs of providing the club good, which is not zero. In the case of broadcasting, the marginal cost of consumption may be zero, but the fixed costs of production are not. Note here that the conventional idea of variable costs is not relevant: although a broadcaster can increase or decrease its costs, once a programme is made, the output 'exists' – it is broadcast, and the marginal cost in respect of an individual consumer is zero.

The way in which the fixed costs are spread across club members matters because, for efficiency reasons, it should not distort the marginal consumption decisions of its members. Typically, a uniform charge is applied, equal to the total costs divided by the number of members. Even here, however, there is a disincentive effect.

Clubs are imperfect solutions, in that, although the marginal cost of use is zero, the club may still exclude some with small positive utility: some people are deterred by the cost of the membership fee and hence are excluded. Clever pricing, such as discounted membership fees for the elderly and young, and those on benefits, can minimise the impact.

---

9   For a survey of club goods, see Sandler & Tschirhart (1997).

Since there are many activities in the economy with public goods characteristics, and because state and voluntary provision suffer from drawbacks and limited funding, it is not surprising that the club solution is a pervasive form of providing public goods. Clubs abound in a host of activities, from professional services (common standards), to sporting activities (common facilities), to Visa cards (common networks). Breakdown services (common back-up networks), journal subscriptions (fixed research costs), childcare clubs (common facilities), the RSPB (common reserves) and the National Trust (common properties) are yet more examples. Most people's wallets and bags are full of membership cards, and direct-debit statements typically list membership fees.

The relevance to public service broadcasting is obvious: the licence fee represents a membership fee for the services of the BBC and other channels. It excludes those who do not pay. Yet, once paid, the cost of viewing programmes is zero, and hence it maintains the non-rival quality.

Clubs differ from subscriptions in an important way, which affects the ways in which markets may fail to overcome the public goods problem. Subscription to individual programmes or services tends to raise the marginal cost of consumption. The narrower the subscription is to the programme, the greater the violation of the non-rivalry zero marginal cost criterion. Subscription to a whole channel is more efficient, and subscription to broadcasting as a whole is even better from an efficiency perspective.

The practical impact of this bears directly on the design of the licence fee. Narrowing it to the BBC will raise the hurdle slightly; moving to subscription fees for particular services makes the market inefficient; and a per-programme charge is the most inefficient outcome from a public goods perspective.

As we shall see, the club goods perspective on the licence fee has very considerable implications not just for the way the public good is provided, but also for the governance of the BBC. If licence fee payers are *members* of a club, there is a corollary in their ownership and control of its activities. We return to this below in section four.

Monopoly and market power

Much analysis of markets starts with the competitive paradigm, and considers whether particular market is, or could be, competitive. Competition, in this usage, is treated as an absolute criterion. Such thinking surfaces in the Ofcom Phase 1 report. In its application to broadcasting, it is argued that the coming of the digital age will reduce entry barriers, creating the opportunity for a large number of companies to flourish. Market forces, in the context of many competing companies, will then, it is argued, deliver what people want – including many of the niches that public service broadcasting aims to serve. The conventional consumer choice issues will be solved, leaving only *some* residual citizenship failures.

Competition is, however, a complex phenomena. No markets are 'competitive' in the sense of the perfect competition ideal of textbook economics. Markets display varying degrees of competition and there are many dimensions and kinds of competition. The policy question is whether there is *enough* competition to negate the need for intervention and, in the broadcasting case, whether in fact the digital age will bring forward yet more entrants to challenge the incumbents.

The Ofcom Phase 1 report is remarkably optimistic in this regard. But the underlying economics may point in a different direction: the economies of scale and scope in broadcasting are pervasive, and there are powerful reasons why vertical integration may be efficient. Rather than a fragmentation with hosts of new competitors, the digital age may turn out to be characterised by a small number of dominant, vertically integrated players, with very significant barriers to entry.

Why might this be so? First, consider the structure of market access. A small number of platforms dominate access. These are supported by high fixed and sunk costs. The only 'revolutionary' method of access is the Internet, and here, too, there may be concentration in access to delivery. The incumbents seek to protect their sunk costs through vertical integration (a strategy which most infrastructure network businesses have traditionally pursued). They vertically integrate with suppliers – film and sporting rights (where there is also concentration) – and with customers. They create brands which package programmes together. Techniques such as margin support and deep discounting are used.

Given that sport and films tend to play a critical role in attracting viewers, entrants may need access to these in order to develop a market offering. As demonstrated in the sports market, the large broadcasters have very great dominance over the popular sources of programming, to the practical exclusion of entrants. Indeed, so important have sports rights become that there have even been attempts by broadcasters to vertically integrate into sporting companies, notably in football.[10] There is no convincing evidence to suggest that the digital age is likely to radically change this link and its impact on market power.

---

10   For an overview of the economics of the sport market, see the special issue of *Oxford Review of Economic Policy* (2003), and, in particular, Szymanski (2003).

Because markets are concentrated around channels and brands, market share greatly affects the economics of both advertising and subscription. Advertising is a sunk and fixed-cost production activity, averaged over the audience. There are therefore powerful reasons for targeting mass audiences and encouraging broadcasters to focus their programmes accordingly. Programme production may have some elements of economies of scale too, as do many sporting activities. These markets have also concentrated, again with football as an obvious example. Though there are many fringe film companies and independent programme makers, these activities, too, have many of the characteristics of oligopolistic competition.

The economies of scope and scale in production, the fixed and sunk costs in platforms, and the sunk costs in advertising will – both separately and in aggregate – mean that the market will not produce optimal diversity. Rather, the oligopolistic competition for market share which results will tend to reduce diversity both in the type of programme and in scheduling. Programme schedules will tend to converge in both content and broadcast timing. These pressures are witnessed in the claims about 'dumbing down' and the perception that, despite the number of channels, the choice is quite limited – hence, the emphasis on 'choice' and 'diversity' in debates about the future of broadcasting.

So what will happen with digitalisation? Market developments are uncertain, and hence no policy should be designed on the assumption that one possible outcome will arise. It is in the nature of competition that there will be surprises. The uncertainty should condition public policy. It may be that the market does turn out to be richly competitive in many dimensions (as Ofcom believes), or it may turn out to continue to be dominated by an oligopoly. If intervention continued to support public service broadcasting in the current way, but Ofcom turned out to be right, and digitalisation led to the competitive outcome, intervention could then be gradually withdrawn. But now suppose the opposite, that there is a tendency towards concentration, but policy assumes competition. In this case, the licence fee and the BBC might have been dismantled, reinforcing the concentration in the market. It would be very hard *ex post* to dismantle an even bigger BSkyB, or to resurrect ITV if it were squeezed out of the market.

Thus, although it is beyond the scope of this essay to provide detailed cost analyses or predict in detail how digitalisation will shape the market, there are some good *general* reasons for thinking that concentration has underlying economic motives and that the dismantling of one competitor (the BBC) will not necessarily be replaced by several new ones. The digital age will bring many surprises, and may lead to an explosion of competition. But it may not, and if policy allowed a round of consolidation and at the same time reduced the status of the BBC, it would probably be irreversible.

The conventional 'solution' to market power is competition policy: many markets display market power and are subject to the constraints of competition law – not to engage in anti-competitive behaviour or to abuse dominance. These constraints will apply here too, but they are unlikely to be sufficient, since the issues relate to structure as well as conduct, and there is little evidence that the competition authorities are willing to contemplate the unbundling of BSkyB. The public good characteristics are one of the major reasons for market power (because the marginal costs are very low, relative to the average costs), and hence have structural implications. Competition policy focused on conduct will not make the underlying economics of structure go away, and hence some form of sectoral policy will be needed to reinforce general competition law.

It is therefore not surprising that Ofcom pulled back from the more conventional economic model that pervaded its Phase 1 report, and in the Phase 2 report opted for a more limited approach instead. Rather than tackling the structure head on, it proposed two incremental additional elements of competition: the new PSP with a focus on new delivery systems, and a greater role for independent productions in the BBC's outputs.

As checks on the BBC's market power, neither element is likely to have significant impact. But having rejected substantive *structural* change, Ofcom opted to constrain the BBC's output towards public sector broadcasting, in effect suggesting that the BBC should exit mass markets that others in the digital age can produce. According to Ofcom's approach, the BBC should retreat from core film and sports markets. Such recommendations not only have the incidental effect of *increasing* BSkyB's market share (and hence may not actually increase anything in the market *as a whole*), but also reflect the narrow economic concept of public service broadcasting, which was criticised above. Add to this the suggested cost squeeze, and the net impact would be for a *gradual* erosion of the BBC's role, and, with it, the *gradual* marginalisation of public sector broadcasting.

The final consideration is how the public good failures interact with market power. Will dominant companies produce the diversity and richness that the citizen and public good arguments point towards? In part, this is a competition issue too: Ofcom rightly points to the benefits of a large number of independent producers challenging the incumbents' programme-making. However, there is also the issue of the brand as a whole, and whether the BBC in particular is able to cross-subsidise within its portfolio of programmes to focus on those with significant public service broadcasting content, even if, as a result, smaller minority audiences are catered for at the expense of mass audiences. The answer depends in large measure upon the method of finance: whether it is licence fee-based, as opposed to being based on advertising or on per-programme charges. This is examined in section five below. But, before we turn to finance – and its relation to market failures – we first need to consider governance and regulation.

4. Government and regulatory failure: the design of intervention and the role of the BBC

The fact that markets fail does not, in itself, mandate intervention. All markets fail: the issue is whether the market failures are greater than the costs of intervention. These costs, referred to as government and regulatory failure, in turn depend upon the design of the intervention.[11] In the broadcasting market, the main interventions are the BBC's institutional structure, the licence fee and the ancillary regulatory framework.

The BBC is a unique institution, designed for a quite different pre-Second World War context, where competition was absent. The broadcasting technology was new and the ways it would evolve uncertain. It was set up as a public corporation and with a governance structure designed to pursue the public interest. It was a structure not unlike that adopted for a broad range of public bodies: its board would decide for itself, within a broad discretionary context, how to interpret the public interest. It would be made up as it went along, in the classic British, pragmatic and empirical approach to administration, regulation and public provision. Governors would be the arbiters of what the corporation would produce. The first director general set out the vision of public service broadcasting – the Reithian approach – which has endured ever since, and proved remarkably adaptable to the changing marketplace.

As a structure, the BBC has certain advantages. It has a history and a corporate culture that define a set of professional ethics, which do not have to be directed. A common culture is often managerially efficient: it takes years to create, and can be quickly dissipated. The BBC has the further advantage that it is largely vertically integrated. In its early history, this was an essential feature of

11 There is a host of different kinds of government and regulatory failures, which can be divided for analytical ease into informational failures, public monopoly failures, and regulatory capture. All of these may pertain to the relationship between the government and the BBC, and none is obviously 'solved' by the existence of Governors.

broadcasting development, but as the market developed the same standards could be applied throughout the full vertical chain.

Such a culture can degenerate into the pursuit of the quiet life. A monopoly position tends to encourage cost inflation, and hence there is a need for effective regulation. This is currently largely provided by the BBC itself, through its Governors. These people are supposed to represent the public interest, and to protect the independence and impartiality of the BBC. Where direct state provision and/or regulation – or, indeed, voluntary provisions – might well have biased its output, the Governors have managed to keep the political process at arms' length, and withstood repeated challenges by politicians of both parties. It is a structure that has arguably performed this role quite well in comparison to many other public institutions and other models internationally.

Yet questions remain. How can we be sure that the BBC is cost-efficient, without the disciplines of competition? The answer is that we cannot, and there is a good argument for an element of external audit. In other core monopolies, this function is performed by independent regulators. These bodies use benchmark and comparative information to assess the efficient cost levels, and prices are set accordingly. While there have been repeated efficiency audits with the past reviews of the BBC, and many internal efficiency drives, there is no such arm's-length regulator, and a good case can be made for passing this efficiency function to Ofcom, with the remit to advise the Secretary of State on this aspect of setting future licence fees. In its Phase 2 report, Ofcom recognises this role, though the claim that efficiency gains might be sufficient to make significant inroads into the licence fee is more a conjecture that a carefully researched empirical proposition.

The question of 'independence' of the BBC in its choice of programmes and editing processes is more difficult, and it is far from clear that Ofcom has a role here. The political dimension of independence can be expressed in economic terms as how to separate the principal (the government) from the agent (the BBC). The recent Hutton Inquiry cast considerable light on the issues, but less on the appropriate structures. In practical terms, the question is: what stands between the government and the BBC? This role is currently fulfilled by the Charter and the Governors. Given the administrative approach of delegating discretion to them, it matters greatly *who they are*, *how they are chosen*, and *how they are held to account*.

If the regulatory task in respect of efficiency is delegated to Ofcom, as suggested above, the Governors' prime functions are to represent the interests of the citizens as listeners and viewers and to ensure that the output is consistent with these interests. It is a role similar to that of the board of the National Trust – representing the members who pay the membership fee, in this case the licence fee. But, unlike the National Trust, the licence fee payers do not elect their representatives, and hence the link is indirect via the political process. It is far from obvious that this is appropriate, and the aim of limiting government and regulatory failure suggests that alternative arrangements should at least be considered. The club good model discussed above provides the basis for one more radical model: creating a direct link to trustees, who could be subject to members' influence and even control. This would take the politics out of the process of selecting Governors, although the sheer size of the resulting BBC membership might limit their effective control.[12]

'Independence' is not a single dimension of conduct. A broadcaster has to *choose* what to broadcast and how to present issues, ideas and arguments. This is not some analytical or abstract activity: the choices made influence and reflect society as a whole. The BBC is required to be 'impartial', but what this means and what it is impartial about are deeply embedded within the political and social context. Referring back to the discussion on the role of citizenship and the extent to which market failure can capture most, or indeed all, of the public service broadcasting concept, independence is not simply a matter of reflecting consumer preferences. It is not simply what consumers would be willing or able to pay for. What sort of independence is produced depends critically on how the institution is designed, its history and the accountability of its programme makers. The club model has the merit of separating out the membership fee from individual programmes, leaving the trustees to make individual output decisions. But it creates a more direct bond with its members than does the BBC Governors' model.

There is an alternative and more radical regulatory model than that discussed above, based on the approach towards telecoms and other network utility services.[13] The BBC could be vertically unbundled and subject to a full economic regulatory regime (rather than just an efficiency audit), driven by Ofcom. This approach has many attractions, inducing consistency between the broadcasters, providing a basis for promoting competition, and, in using an existing regulatory body, keeping the costs of regulation down. It is also implicit in the Ofcom Phase 2 report.

---

12 Although its governance has been subject to criticism, the National Trust manages to enfranchise over 3 million members.

13 See Laffont & Tirole (1999) for a comprehensive survey of the telecommunications issues, and in particular the discussion of universal service in Chapter 6.

There are, however, problems with the utility model. First, unbundling would need to be an industry policy, not BBC-specific. It makes little sense to break up the BBC without also breaking up the other players, notably BSkyB. To do one, but not the other, would reinforce the market power of BSkyB and hence the overall level of competition is unlikely to be improved, and may actually fall. But since nobody is actually proposing to tackle BSkyB in this way, the unbundling of the BBC on its own is unlikely to be desirable.

Bringing the BBC under the full wing of Ofcom has several advantages. Ofcom has expertise in respect of competition and competition policy, and in the broadcasting market. If the purpose of Ofcom is to bring consistency to regulation across broadcasting and communications, then having a domain over the whole market might be a sensible step. Again, however, there are practical problems. The BBC would not need Governors and Ofcom to play the regulatory role: the Governors, as currently constituted, would be redundant, and the BBC would have a normal corporate board instead, even if it remained not-for-profit. As with unbundling, halfway houses may be more imperfect than the *status quo*.

5. Financing public service broadcasting and the licence fee

The licence fee as a method of finance was devised in a world where the BBC was the monopoly provider. It was therefore a fee for access to a service, and for pragmatic reasons was tied to the ownership of radios and televisions. There are good economic reasons for thinking that this was very efficient: it was a classic club membership fee, which recovered the costs of the networks from the users without significantly distorting marginal decisions. Given that the marginal cost was zero, as discussed above, it provided the right incentives to viewers. In the monopoly world, then, the licence fee was optimal.

This early justification was undermined by the arrival of competitors. By tying the licence fee to radio and television ownership, in principle viewers might be paying for a service they did not want, although, in practice, everyone watched the two main channels. While audience share has fallen, it can be assumed that almost all watch at least some BBC output or tune in to one or more BBC radio stations. Whether the proceeds of the licence fee should accrue to one supplier, however, is a more open question.

Two other forms of finance have been suggested on numerous occasions: advertising and subscription. The main economic issues in relation to advertising as the principal source of finance have been well researched. Advertising has the advantage of avoiding direct payment by viewers, and therefore does not distort the incentives to watch programmes. The marginal cost is therefore zero. It therefore allows the public good characteristics to be met. However, this does not mean that it is costless – the costs will be passed through to the consumers of the products. Advertising is itself a market with considerable failures, as noted above. It is a sunk cost, and there are scale economies. If the objective of the BBC were to maximise advertising revenues, it would shape its outputs to maximise the benefits to the advertisers rather than the viewers. It would encourage convergence on mass-audience programmes and hence undermine public service broadcasting.

Advertising can also create disutility: viewers do not choose to watch adverts and, for some programmes – particularly live events – the disutility can be quite large. Finally, advertising will have a consequence for competition in the market. If the BBC were to switch to this form of finance, the ITV companies would lose advertising revenues, and hence the quality of their programming would decline. There may even be a reduction in the number of mass-market channels.

Direct charges, in the form of subscriptions, for programmes or channels split up a market, and have their own transaction costs associated with the exclusion mechanisms. A charge-per-programme creates an important negative externality: each person paying the charge contributes to the fixed cost. Hence, as the number of viewers reduces, the price per programme rises to meet the total costs. As a result, the gap between marginal and average cost increases, reducing the access. This effect is likely to be especially important in the case of minority public service broadcasting.

A per-channel charge is more likely to encourage diversity, since it spreads the average cost of all the programmes over the subscribers. As such, it is rather like the licence fee, except that it excludes between channels. To the extent that all customers might want to benefit from the lower average costs created by the fact that the licence fee covers all viewers, as opposed to a higher licence fee if some defect, the economic balance of costs and benefits in this regard is complex. What needs to be compared is the benefits to consumers who would be in the margin between the two levels of licence fee: the 'everyone' level and the 'channel' level. Since these are likely to be people constrained off through lack of income, consideration of social issues may tip the balance to the all-channels licence fee approach.

6. Conclusions: a case for pragmatic, not revolutionary reforms

This essay has considered two main aspects of the debate on the future of the BBC: the case for public service broadcasting, and the case for the licence fee.

In the process it has considered some of the arguments for the *status quo*: leaving the BBC roughly as it is, and the licence fee as a universal all-channels charge.

The case for public broadcasting should be based on values which go beyond mere economic efficiency – indeed, the citizen argument differs from the economic in that the former treats everyone equally, while the latter treats people according to their income constraints. An economically efficient broadcasting market, which pays proper regard to the market failures, will not be the most desirable if citizens-based arguments count.

Nevertheless, market failures cannot be ignored, and the pervasiveness of public goods and market power transcends the coming of the digital age. Ofcom's assertion that digital technology will change the nature of the public service broadcasting debate is probably correct only at the margin: in the digital age, the public good characteristics do not go away, nor will market power. Indeed, there are some good reasons to believe that the public good characteristics could make per-programme payments highly disadvantageous to marginal low-income viewers, and may actually reduce choice because the average cost of minority programmes will rise as the number of viewers fall. Without the BBC in roughly its current form, the market may actually concentrate further.

These considerations lead to the following conclusions: that there is a strong case for intervening to encourage the provision of public service broadcasting; that the licence fee remains an appropriate method of finance; and that the BBC should continue to play the central role in correcting for the market failures. Although the Phase 1 report points against this, in Phase 2 Ofcom broadly accepts these conclusions. It is more likely to deliver the citizen benefits than other alternatives, since, by including everyone in the contributions to the average costs, the gap between average and marginal costs will be minimised.

However, there may still be some marginal citizens excluded at the current level of the licence fee, and here there are two solutions: direct social security to provide the income, or some form of special category with lower charges. The latter route has many advantages, although it has to be carefully crafted to achieve the trade-off between maximising the number of contributors to the average costs, and not deterring people at the margin.

None of these considerations, however, implies that the BBC's current organisational structure and the domain of its programming and activities are optimal. There are also good general reasons to believe that it lacks incentives to be cost-efficient. Ofcom, in Phase 2, suggests a number of remedies, though none is convincing. The proposed PSP competitor and the greater reliance on independents are, at best, marginal, and, in the case of the PSP, may actually be ineffective in the context of the BBC's substantial website public services. More worrying still is Ofcom's suggestion that the BBC should be constrained to a narrow version of public service broadcasting, and hence retreat from the film and sports markets, thereby reducing choice and increasing BSkyB's market power.

That leaves the crucial requirement of effective governance and regulation. The question of who decides what the public interest is – and hence what best meets the public service broadcasting requirements – is wrapped up in the governance structure, and it is far from clear that the current internalisation of this problem is necessarily optimal. Although much of this essay – and the wider debate – has been about market failure, the issues around government and regulatory failure are of considerable importance, and once many of the former have been resolved, the Charter Review will need to look closely at the latter.

Bringing the economics of market failure – particularly public goods, the method of finance and the governance – together into a coherent framework can be achieved by thinking of the BBC as, in essence, a club. A club internalises the public good aspects efficiently by maximising access through minimising marginal costs, and the licence fee can be regarded as an (imperfect) form of club fee. In the BBC's case, what is missing from this framework is a direct link between the licence fee payers (the club members) and the BBC. It has been argued in this essay that there is merit in thinking about the role of Governors as close to that of trustees – what might be called the 'National Trust model' – and exploring greater accountability to, and control by, its members.

References

Broome, J. (1999), *Ethics out of Economics*, Cambridge: Cambridge University Press.

Cohen, G. A. (1995), *Self-Ownership, Freedom and Equality*, Cambridge: Cambridge University Press.

Dasgupta, P. (2001), *Human Well-Being and the Natural Environment*, Oxford: Oxford University Press.

Davies, G. (2004), 'Economics and the BBC Charter', lecture at the Saïd Business School, Oxford, June 10th. A version of this lecture is published as Chapter 7 of this book.

HM Treasury (2004), *Science and Innovation Investment Framework 2004–2014*, July, London: Stationery Office.

Laffont, J.-J. and Tirole, T. (1999), *Competition in Telecommunications*, Cambridge MA: MIT Press.

Marquand, D. (2004), *Decline of the Public*, Cambridge: Polity Press.

Myles, G. D. (1995), *Public Economics*, Cambridge: Cambridge University Press.

Ofcom (2004a), *Ofcom Review of Public Service Television Broadcasting: Phase 1 – Is Television Special?*, Office of Communications.

Ofcom (2004b), Ofcom *Review of Public Service Television Broadcasting: Phase 2 – Meeting the Digital Challenge?*, Office of Communications.

Sandler, T. and Tschirhart, J. (1997), 'Club Theory: Thirty Years Later', *Public Choice*, **93**:3, 335–55.

Sen, A.K. (1979), 'Personal Utilities and Public Judgements', *The Economic Journal*, **89**:355, 537–58.

Szymanski, S. (2003), 'The Economics of Sport', *Oxford Review of Economic Policy*, **19**:4, 467–77.

2

The Public Realm in Broadcasting

Damian Green

T his is the essay of the book where non-economists can relax. Most of the essays here are written by distinguished economists to illustrate the value of Public Service Broadcasting (PSB) even under the narrow but all-powerful assumptions of that once dismal but now all-conquering science. Proponents of PSB have to engage in the economic arguments, if only to tackle the views of those who take a purely economic view of broadcasting, best epitomised by the former head of the American Federal Communications Commission, Mark Fowler, who said that a TV was 'Just another appliance … a toaster with pictures'. A degree only partly in economics nearly thirty years ago does not qualify me to compete in that company, so I propose to concentrate on the equally important but perhaps more subtle argument about whether a healthy society will still find a need for Public Service Broadcasting, and institutions which exist purely to provide it, in the era when spectrum scarcity has entirely disappeared.

The difference between this essay and others in this book is that it does not seek either to frame an economic justification for PSB, or to translate the arguments it uses into economic concepts. It argues that there are purely non-economic values which can be used to justify PSB, discusses whether these values still hold in the digital world and whether a development of the current mode of funding and producing PSB, through the BBC, will be the most effective in a fully digital environment.

Globalisation
The pros and cons of globalisation are hotly fought in many spheres of economic and political argument, but the cultural effects are less often analysed. In this

regard, Britain is much less sensitive and self-aware than France, where defence of the specific national culture is not only taken for granted as a key aim of public policy, but is aggressively turned into practical politics both through domestic legislation and international agreements. There is a tendency in Britain to sneer at French attempts to protect the national film industry from Hollywood, but it is at least worth pondering whether we would feel equally sensitive if there was a danger that British-made TV programmes would simply disappear to the margins of the schedule on every mainstream channel (Look at the schedule for Sky One as an example of a successful and popular general interest channel which has few British programmes at peak time).

This serves as a practical example of a general point; that in cultural terms globalisation inevitably involves the dilution of national cultures. The degree of dilution will depend on the particular circumstances of each country, and in this regard Britain is particularly vulnerable. The sharing of language, the long-standing close political links and the freedom of access to all markets in the UK has meant that American mass entertainment products have found Britain a receptive market for many decades. Jazz, Hollywood musicals, rock and roll, westerns and cop shows have come and (and in some cases) gone, but their cultural imprint has stayed. Recent TV schedules featuring *Friends*, *The Sopranos*, *The Simpsons* and *The West Wing* show that the influence is still strong, and has if anything moved up market.

The influence of American culture has been so pervasive for so long that it almost goes unnoticed. What is happening now in certain sections of British life is that cultures from other parts of the world are coming to be equally available. The traditional journey of immigrant groups has been away from their country or region of origin in cultural terms, so that as the generations pass they feel fewer ties to a non-British background. The easy availability of, for example, Arabic language TV channels displaying a view of the world very different from the mainstream UK media allows individuals and groups who live here to separate themselves from mainstream discourse much more easily than before. The paradoxical effect of globalisation in this instance is not that every country becomes more like every other country, but that groups within each country find it easier to live their lives entirely separately from the surrounding culture.

In many cases, this is purely a matter of choice which a democratic society can accommodate. Clearly in some instances, if the separated community is hostile to the agreed norms of behaviour in the country it will cause problems. But even if that particularly dangerous condition does not exist (as it does not in Britain today) a healthy society will only exist if there are some general norms of behaviour and attitude which are universally shared. So even if a society is happy to permit and indeed promote diversity there must be a common core of values which are available to all citizens, and, equally importantly, universally available means of discussing and developing these values.

This is a key role for Public Service Broadcasting, (and indeed Public Service Narrowcasting – of which more later) in a digital environment. The provision of programmes which attract mass audiences and which promote the expression of specific UK culture – and also specific national and local cultures within the UK – is a highly desirable phenomenon. In this form, PSB not only helps ward off the prospect of Britain developing a purely sub-American mass culture, which even Americophiles should regret unless they have given up on national identity altogether, but also ensures that an accessible alternative is available for those who would otherwise retreat purely into another culture.

The role of PSB in disseminating and shaping a British cultural identity goes well beyond the up-market roles of giving impartial news and current affairs coverage and offering high culture in a way that the market would not necessarily provide. Indeed once digital services are universally available there is an argument that offering mass-appeal distinctly British content becomes the most important part of the public service remit. All three of the Reithian trinity of information, education and entertainment will be available from more suppliers in the digital age. Each of the three will need to be available with a uniquely British accent if British culture is not to be heavily diluted, and those offering British content must have the talent and distribution networks to ensure that the vast majority of the population regularly want to and can receive it. So popular content is at least as important as 'difficult' content.

Britishness

Of course, for this analysis to be valid there must be a British culture which is both recognisably distinctive and worth preserving. This is not the vehicle for a full discussion of the fascinating subject of what it means to be British in the early 21st century, but it is important to observe that this debate is being conducted with an energy and passion which shows that Britishness is a valuable, if elusive, concept which politicians and citizens want preserved. The two points on which all commentators agree is that the speed with which Britishness is evolving is faster than ever before, and that British culture is becoming increasingly variegated. The philosopher John Gray wrote:

> The national culture of Britain today is not a seamless garment, woven from a single cloth, but a patchwork quilt, whose beauty lies in its

complexity. The common culture of Britain today cannot be other than pluralist – in terms of ethnicity, lifestyle and world-view. It is at least doubtful if the depth and subtlety of cultural diversity in Britain today can be articulated in market-led broadcasting services which do not have a competitor that is different in kind – public service broadcasting.[1]

The aspects of British life which the people themselves have long valued, such as tolerance, fairness, open-mindedness and inventiveness, can be expressed in different ways as times change, and popular culture will reflect this. In one era, Colonel Blimp helped make a set of ideas impossible to hold in respectable society. In another, Viz magazine's Sid the Sexist performed the same function. The combination of a dislike for ignorant prejudice, the use of humour, and a quiet pride in a society which does not tolerate that prejudice, is as 'typically British' today as it was 60 years ago. This is only one example of the permanent values which infuse British society and culture and which can only be effectively shared if there are indigenous creative industries remaking them for each generation.

The arrival of the digital age makes the task of those creative industries easier, in that consumers can find many more ways of enjoying the content. At the same time, that part of the creative community which has public service obligations faces a more difficult job. Digital technology does not recognise national boundaries. If you type a word into an internet search engine you have to make a positive effort to generate UK sites. As the availability of video online becomes the norm, and as the functions of different types of screen merge, this type of searching will become more common for video content. So if we value British culture then we must make a positive effort to ensure that there is popular content available on digital media which reflects and enhances it. The content will need to be strong enough on its own account to create a mass audience. The old skills of scheduling are becoming obsolete, so attempting to lead audiences into byways which they did not know they wanted to explore will no longer work. There are new difficulties facing public service broadcasters.

Nevertheless, the sheer choice of entertainment from around the world makes it desirable for there to be strong cultural bodies with purely British interests that engage as widely as possible with all groups in society. These bodies should seek to maintain existing cultural bindings and create new ones. There is some evidence that one way this can be done is to use imaginative ways to present

---

1   Gray J. (1993) 'Cultural Diversity, National Identity and the Case for Public Service Broadcasting Britain', in W. Stevenson (ed.) *All our Futures*. London: BFI Publishing.

existing cultural events for a new audience. The best example of this is the *Last Night of the Proms*. Few national events can be so steeped in a traditional display of patriotism. The BBC has sensibly resisted temptation (and pressure) to change this and has greatly increased awareness of the *Proms* through its *Proms in the Park* in Belfast, Glasgow, Swansea, Manchester and London. 90 per cent of the UK population are now aware of the *Proms*. The average audience for a Prom concert on BBC Two in 2004 was 1.2 million – 30 per cent more than the average classical concert. For the *Last Night of the Proms* the TV audience was nearly five million.

The *Proms* is an annual event, but the same sort of effect can be seen from less regular broadcasts. Even with the fragmentation of audiences with the multiplicity of channels, broadcasting can bring people together to share an event. England v Portugal in Euro 2004 was watched by just under 24 million people. Within these mass audiences, the BBC has not lost its pulling power. The Millennium countdown saw 10.6 million watching the BBC with 2.7 million watching ITV. There is also the chance to create a community of interest. Programmes such as *Restoration*, *Great Britons* and *The Big Read* show that mass audiences can be created for events where the audience is involved in the outcome, and that these programmes need not be standard 'reality TV' fare.

In the digital age institutions which promote British cultural binding will be as worthy of public support as other public services such as parks and museums. To return to John Gray:

> The goods produced by broadcasting are cultural goods – they belong to the category of inherently public goods which enter into a common form of life within which individual choice becomes meaningful and worthwhile. In this they are like the streets and parks of a well-ordered city in the classical European tradition. Of course, streets and parks are not public goods in the technical terms of economic theory. They can be viewed as, and may indeed become, private consumer goods, paid for by those who use them, and designed to exclude those who do not pay. When this happens, however, a great public good is lost – that of city life itself, with its public places for loitering and sauntering, no less than for getting speedily from place to place.[2]

This is a good analogy for broadcasting in a digital age. Consumers have a huge number of avenues they can explore, or use for different purposes at different

2   Gray J. (1993).

times. What is important for a society is to ensure that in those avenues are attractive destinations which are universally available and which make a contribution towards promoting the shared ideals of the society. Because of the particular vulnerability of UK culture to domination by the US entertainment giants, whose vast home market gives them the opportunity to provide programming which is relatively cheap when it arrives here, the need for Britain to ensure a competitive domestic production industry is highly important.

As spectrum scarcity disappears, the ability of Ofcom to ensure that commercial broadcasters can be implicitly subsidised to provide public service programming is disappearing. For the last 50 years the scarcity value of the analogue spectrum has meant that non-BBC broadcasters can be charged a fee for its use and still have enough left over both to fulfil public service obligations and make a profit. By the end of this decade this scarcity value will be drastically reduced, and will disappear altogether in the course of the next decade. So looking to the existing commercial broadcasters for public service content will be increasingly futile, unless we move to explicit and transparent subsidies to private operators. Channel 4, a highly successful example of a commercial broadcaster which has combined a defined public service remit with a total lack of explicit cash subsidy in the analogue era, is arguing that this happy combination cannot continue after analogue switch-off. Combine this thought with the likely effects on the British broadcasting ecology of a purely market financed system, and the need for an acceptable method and level of subsidy to maintain public service programming is obvious.

Public service broadcasting and social capital[3]

Why is it necessary to promote this national cultural identity? Why should we care about the cultural binding that it helps bring about? The current academic debate which is most relevant is on the issue of social capital. Robert Putnam, one of the prominent writers on this subject, defines social capital as 'features of social life – networks, norms, and trust – that enable participants to act together more effectively to pursue shared objectives'.[4] Francis Fukuyama has produced a more expanded definition:

> Social Capital can be defined simply as a set of informal values or norms shared among members of a group that permits cooperation among them.

---

3   This section owes much to Brookes, M. (2004) *Watching Alone – Social capital and public service broadcasting*. The Work Foundation in partnership with the BBC.

4   Putnam, R. D. (1995) 'Tuning in, tuning out: The strange disappearance of social capital in America', *Political Science and Politics*, Vol. 28.

If members of the group come to expect that others will behave reliably and honestly, then they will come to trust one another. Trust is like a lubricant that makes the running of any group or organisation more efficient.[5]

The economic effect of a more trusting society can be measurable. The higher the level of social capital, the higher the long-term rate of economic growth and the better the performance in other measures of well-being.

Within this theory different types of social capital can be discerned. Bonding capital supports bonds within groups which are already homogeneous, such as families. Bridging capital provides links with more distant friends or acquaintances. Linking capital refers to relations between groups which may otherwise have little in common, such as social classes.

Inevitably, television has featured in the literature on social capital. The orthodox view is that TV is one of the factors of modern life which destroys social capital by promoting solitary and passive activities. These in turn reduce the amount of habitual interaction and therefore cut the number of opportunities to develop trust. Putnam himself is a leading proponent of this view, linking the decline in membership of groups with high TV viewing. In his most famous work *Bowling Alone: The Collapse and Revival of American Community* Putnam quotes T.S Eliot saying of television that 'It is a medium of entertainment which permits millions of people to listen to the same joke at the same time and yet remain lonesome' (Putnam 2000).

This is a misreading of TV at its best. It can and does provide many of the shared experiences which bring together the highest number of people in advanced societies. This is particularly true of PSB, which explicitly aims at this. One of the ironies of the debate over the future of PSB is that broadcast TV has turned full circle in 50 years in its perceived effect on the values of British society. When it first grew to pre-eminence in the 1950s it was regarded by the high-minded with horror – it was the 'idiot's lantern'. In the digital world it may be the best weapon not only to ensure the transmission of traditional high culture beyond a small elite, but also to promote the sharing of national values.

The ways in which PSB can add to social capital are various. The need for news and comment which is not already aimed at the viewer's particular prejudices is important to enable public discourse to continue in a non-polarised way. Already

5   Fukuyama, F. (1999) *The Great Disruption – Human nature and the Reconstitution of Social Order.* Free Press.

in the US there is a perception that certain TV networks are basically conservative or liberal, and viewers with particular inclinations can choose broadcasters who reflect their existing view. In radio this process is even further advanced. As the relative importance of the internet as a primary source of news and information increases, the tendency to choose news sources that fit already existing views will be increased.

This already happens with newspaper reading, so why should it be so damaging if electronic media follow? The problem is summed up by what the American academic Cass Sunstein has called the 'Law of group polarisation'.[6] This shows that after discussions inside a group where participants broadly agree on an issue, opinions are shifted to the more extreme views within the group. So if media outlets which attempt, however imperfectly, to represent different opinions are replaced by one-sided outlets society will fragment into groups which hold increasingly hostile and extreme views towards each other. The whole of public discourse will come to resemble the hunting debate, where those who care passionately on both sides are polarised to a degree which makes rational argument difficult and acceptable compromise impossible. The fact that the market will provide a choice of outlets which allow any view to have an airing will not promote debate in the way PSB does, because the different sides on any issue will literally not be listening to each other.

The potential for long-term damage to democratic society if this were allowed to happen is clear. Unlike in many other countries we have a tradition of electronic media which are not tied to one political party or one set of interest groups. This is a valuable part of our heritage which it is worth fighting to preserve in the digital age. There are many factors tending to reduce the amount of glue which holds our society together. Those institutions which help bind us together are worth preserving.

One other related issue is the type of mass audience programmes that are produced by different types of broadcasters. Those who believe that PSB should only consist of programmes which would not be provided by the market criticise the BBC for chasing ratings with popular programmes. Indeed, this has been presented as a paradox for public funding: the BBC only justifies public funding if it provides programmes which the free market would not; at the same time it only justifies public funding if everyone wants to watch or listen to its output; in other words, if it provides the popular programming the free market would

---

6   Sunstein, C.R. (1999) 'The Law of Group Polarization', *Law and Economics Working Paper No. 91*, University of Chicago Law School.

provide anyway. The way out of this paradox is to see whether the current system of PSB (including ITV under the current regulatory regime) does provide all the types of popular programming that are desirable. This discussion is often conducted in terms of programme genres. It is important to look at it from another angle in our more diverse society. What we need is not just a large audience but programming which both creates a mass audience and builds up that mass audience from different sectors of society.

As an example, take the popularity of programmes within different ethnic groups. The difference between US and British TV is stark. In the US only one programme comes into the top ten of both white and black viewers. Seven of the ten most popular programmes for black Americans are among the least popular for white audiences. By contrast, of the top ten programmes for whites and ethnic minorities in the UK in 2002, five featured in both lists. This suggests that British TV, with its large element of public service obligations, is significantly more successful at creating social capital than American TV. Other ways of cutting the cake show similar successes for British TV. Martin Brookes has shown that *EastEnders* is watched by around 50 per cent of viewers within every social class (its viewing figures among ABs are 49 per cent, if you are reading this and feeling uneasy about being a fan). More than 40 per cent of every age group watches *EastEnders*, with figures ranging from 44 per cent among those over 65 to 71 per cent among 16–24 year olds.[7] So this example of precisely the type of programme which would be taken off the BBC by those who take a narrow definition of public service broadcasting is a massive and regular shared experience across age groups, social classes and ethnic groups. It is part of the glue which helps keep modern Britain together. As such, it would seem perverse to put it at risk as we move to the digital age.

The BBC's future role

If we accept that the creation of social capital and the promotion of cultural ties as part of national identity are good things, and that PSB is likely to be an effective tool for pursuing these goals in the digital age, the next question is whether the BBC, in its existing or a modified form, is the best way to fulfil this aim.

One argument in favour is a purely pragmatic one: the best existing tool to hand to promote this cultural binding is the BBC. The Ofcom review of public service TV (Ofcom 2004a, 2004b) is highly relevant at this point, as it is the best

---

7   Brookes, M. (2004) p. 34.

contemporary study of audience attitudes to the BBC and PSB more generally. The background to these audience studies is Ofcom's own thinking that in the digital age PSB should be defined in terms of purposes and characteristics rather than specific types of programming. These purposes would be:

- To inform ourselves and others and to increase our understanding of the world;

- To stimulate our interest and knowledge of the arts, science, history and other topics;

- To reflect and strengthen our cultural identity;

- To make us aware of different cultures and alternative viewpoints.[8]

To fulfil this specification, PSB programmes would need distinctive characteristics. They would be:

- High quality, being well-funded and well produced;

- Original, having new UK content, rather than being repeats or acquired from abroad;

- Innovative, developing new ideas and reworking existing approaches, rather than copying old ones;

- Challenging, making viewers think;

- Engaging, continuing to be accessible and enjoyable for viewers; and

- Widely available – if the content is publicly funded, as many people as possible should have the chance to watch it.[9]

Ofcom also believes that plurality of supply is vital to preserve these public service characteristics, and that therefore we need more than one large PSB provider, as well as an open system of commissioning which means that a wide range of producers are involved in making public service programmes. Within this framework, indeed 'at the heart' of it, Ofcom wants to see a 'well-funded BBC producing distinctive and high-quality programming'.[10] The key to this is clearly the funding levels and mechanism for paying. Perhaps the most surprising aspect of the Ofcom findings is that people prefer to pay collectively

8   Ofcom (2004b), p. 110.
9   Ibid.
10 Ibid, p. 96.

for their PSB rather than through a subscription. Despite the success and popularity of Sky subscription systems, viewers still regard a licence fee as an appropriate way of paying for the BBC.

So the licence fee, surprisingly in a historical context, still has validity. Licence fee evasion has been brought down from year to year, from 8.8 per cent in 2001 to 5.7 per cent in 2004. It seems that the licence fee is a popular poll tax, and you can only imagine the sense of awe and wonder with which a politician types those words. Even more surprisingly, there is no desire from the public for a cut in the licence fee. Viewers would be willing to pay around £150 to receive the full array of PSB which they currently enjoy, according to an Ofcom report based on research from MORI.[11] This is roughly the current licence fee plus the implicit subsidy available to other companies with public service obligations. The BBC has done its own research which paints an even more encouraging picture about the public willingness to pay. The research carried out by the BBC and Human Capital[12] (see Chapter 4) found that:

- 81 per cent would be willing to pay the current level of around £10 per month;

- 60 per cent said they would pay £15 per month;

- 42 per cent said they would pay £20 per month;

- 19 per cent said they would pay £30 per month;

- 9 per cent said they would pay £49 per month.

It may be that the Ofcom research failed to capture a public willingness to pay significant amounts more to preserve the services now on offer from the BBC. This level of support may stem from a knowledge of the widespread nature of BBC services. Certainly Ofcom's detailed research into how people use TV backs up the thesis that it is not simply a form of mindless relaxation. 71 per cent say it is their main source of entertainment. But 55 per cent say it is their main source of news and 58 per cent say it is their chief source of knowledge about science, nature and history.[13] Interestingly, even in the growing number of multi-channel households there was strong support for channels which aimed at high-minded objectives. These figures should not be used as an argument for the

---

11 Ofcom (2004b), pp. 47–51.

12 BBC/Human Capital (2004) *Measuring the Value of the BBC – A report by the BBC and Human Capital*. BBC.

13 Ofcom (2004a), p. 48.

status quo as there are significant problems emerging for mainstream PSB channels. The audience share of the terrestrial channels among 16–34 year olds declined from 84 per cent in 1998 to 69 per cent in 2003, and their share among ethnic minority audiences was down to 56 per cent. Younger audiences and ethnic minorities rarely watched mainstream news output.[14]

So there is a clear challenge for the BBC to justify its range of services, although it is a challenge to be faced against a background of widely held public goodwill. The BBC's response has been to postulate the importance of public value as a justification for its continued existence. The origin of this concept lies in three principles which are common to much public policy, in basic services such as health and education as well as the additional hallmarks of a civilised society such as museums or public parks. These principles are:

- *Universality* – freely available to everyone;

- *Fairness and Equity* – because it is held in common it should reflect the needs and interests of all its different users;

- *Accountability* – the public has the right to monitor the performance and guide the future of the BBC through civic institutions.

The justification for the BBC to continue to receive public subsidy in the digital age is that it will provide public value, which means that it serves audiences not just as consumers but also as members of the wider society. The BBC claims to create public value in five ways[15]:

- *Democratic value:* the BBC supports civic life and national debate by providing trusted and impartial news and information that helps citizens make sense of the world and encourages them to engage with it;

- *Cultural and creative value:* the BBC enriches the UK's cultural life by bringing talent and audiences together to break new ground, to celebrate our cultural heritage, and to broaden the national conversation;

- *Educational value:* by offering audiences of every age a world of formal and informal educational opportunity in every medium, the BBC helps build a society strong in knowledge and skills;

---

14 Ofcom (2004a), p. 44.
15 BBC (2004) *Building public value – Renewing the BBC for a digital world*, p. 30. BBC.

- *Social and community value:* by enabling the UK's many communities to see what they hold in common and how they differ, the BBC seeks to build social cohesion and tolerance through greater understanding;

- *Global value:* the BBC supports the UK's global role by being the world's most trusted provider of international news and information and by showcasing the best of British culture to a global audience.

Faced with such high-minded aspirations, it is tempting to pick on some of the more egregiously populist programming of the Greg Dyke era and ask exactly which of the five types of value are being promoted. That would be (a little) unfair. The 'public value framework' is a serious attempt to provide a non-economic basis against which the BBC's aspirations and performance can be judged in the future, together with a test for assessing its impact on the wider market. If the BBC is to remain at the heart of British TV it must justify its privileged position on a continuous basis, and not simply once every five or ten years when its Charter is up for renewal or facing a mid-term review.

It would of course be possible to try to judge every minute of BBC output against the criteria, but more relevant at this stage is to identify the potential pinch points. The first of these is to what extent the BBC's national aspirations require regional and local manifestations. This is particularly relevant in that Ofcom is proposing to transfer some of the current regional obligations of the ITV companies, notably the non-news regional programming requirement, to the BBC. At present this programming is not highly valued by viewers, but the evidence is that this is mainly because it is not seen as high quality output.

The logic of the shift is that the BBC would be trusted to improve the quality of this genre of programming. As a first principle, it is highly likely that it is impossible to explain Britain to itself without going outside London. So if the BBC wishes to continue to aspire to be the national broadcaster it needs to be based in a number of locations around the country. This will mean creating a critical mass of talent in different cities so that nationally acceptable programming can be produced. One offshoot of this should be a rise in the standard of regional programming. The obvious danger here is dilution. If the BBC attempts to create serious production centres in too many places it will fail to maintain quality. If it concentrates on one or two centres only, other regions may feel neglected. The balance between national and local production is not an easy one, but it will be even more important for the BBC in the digital era as it will be the only UK broadcaster instructed and funded to achieve it.

The next problem is the trade-off between the 'citizen value' of BBC output and its straightforward economic value to consumers. This does not matter to the BBC as an institution but it is vital to other content providers, who already have serious complaints about the BBC crowding them out of certain markets. This has been true in the magazine field, but in the long term it will be most important in terms of websites, where the ability to leverage existing popular content could be the key to commercial success. The only solution to this is tougher regulation of BBC activities than has been the case in the past. I am personally sceptical that the moves proposed to separate the Governors from BBC management will prove sufficient both to guarantee that the BBC is behaving fairly, and to allow its actual and potential rivals the confidence that regulation is tough and effective. The argument is that in commercial activities the BBC is already regulated under normal competition law, so it does not need any special rules. But regulating after the fact is not as effective as preventing abuse in the first place, so even the suspicion that the BBC can lock up a segment of the market will discourage others from trying something new. Any regulatory regime needs to provide certainty for all players in the market. I hope the new governance system works, but I wait to be convinced. What is certain is that a reformed governance system is necessary both to ensure a level commercial playing field and to ensure that the BBC meets its core public service obligations.

One reason why this is so important will be the increasing need for Public Service Narrowcasting. As access to video content spreads across different types of screen and improves in quality as broadband becomes universal, inevitably some public service output will need to be aimed at very specific groups. This does not reduce the importance of the mass appeal PSB discussed above, but will be needed to enhance it if the BBC and other public service providers are to fulfil their mission in a digital environment. So BBC websites will be key both to maintaining the BBC's near-universal reach (a central aspect of public value), and in particular to keeping viewers in those parts of the population which, as we have seen, the BBC finds it increasingly difficult to attract. This is setting the BBC a very difficult task. It must produce websites which meet some or all of the criteria of public value; these sites must be attractive enough and marketed well enough to help the BBC reach all sections of the population; each of the sites must encourage more general engagement with society (to add to social capital); and they must be strictly regulated so they are not trading unfairly with commercial sites – actual or potential.

If we accept that the BBC will need to provide more than traditional radio and TV channels to fulfil its remit in the digital age, then it is clear that regulatory issues will become even more difficult than they have been throughout the BBC's history. They will be necessary in new media areas, where it is impossible to rely on traditional structures. But it is essential that they are addressed now, in the current Charter Review period, both to enable the BBC to plan with confidence and to enable the rest of the UK media industry to know that there are market gaps which they will be allowed to fill without publicly-funded competition.

One final point about how the BBC will help to build public value in the digital age relates to training and skills development. A country like the UK will be increasingly dependent on its creative industries in the decades to come. If I can stray dangerously close to the economic arguments that I am trying to avoid, it has become essential for any advanced country to be clear about which areas of economic activity will provide it with a comparative advantage as the rest of the world progresses ever more quickly through the stages of development. Large parts of what was once called the 'tertiary sector' (service industries) are now done better and more cheaply in other parts of the world. Replacing British coal mines and steel works with call centres proved a very short term expedient. The creative sector is one in which we have a critical mass and a genuine world lead and supporting the institutions which keep it progressing is rational.

For the creative industries to flourish there will need to be a good-sized home market in which new talent can flourish, and a structure of training which allows talents across the board, from purely creative to purely technical, to be developed. In theory, all of this could happen without the BBC, as other players developed their own talent. In practice, one of the comparative advantages the British creative industries have had is an institution like the BBC which has trained successive generations of media workers, most of whom have gone on to work elsewhere. Looking at the wider state of technical training in UK industry, it would be folly for one sector to put at risk its strongest training agent.

All of these are positive recommendations for the future of the BBC. One cautionary point is also required. It is very important that the BBC does not become a monopoly provider of PSB. Important both for the BBC itself, to avoid the classic problems of monopoly, and even more importantly for the rest of us, so that what constitutes public service content in the digital age is open to contestability. Inevitably the question whether any individual piece of content is 'Public Service' is difficult to answer at the margin. In an era when content will be accessed through many different media, each of them providing a slightly different experience as the audiences respond to the same original creative impulse, it will become more difficult to answer.

Therefore it will be necessary for other institutions to be focussed on providing public service content, so that the virtues of plurality can be maintained within the public service sector. Ofcom has suggested a Public Service Publisher, which will receive around £300m of direct public funding every year, but which will not be a traditional channel. It has also described funding Channel 4 directly as 'a credible option', and said it 'stands ready to be corrected' in its hostility to an Arts Council of the Air.[16] Much of the debate in the coming years will concentrate on these options. What is important is that, as viewers, we can continue to have displayed more than one concept of what constitutes Public Service Broadcasting.

Conclusion

The final question to be addressed by this essay is 'How long will the support for PSB last and will it disappear in a fully digital era'? Since this requires a degree of hypothetical thinking it can perhaps better be answered in the essays devoted to economic analysis. But there remains an underlying societal point; the fact that cultural binding becomes if anything more important as the ability to transmit information and opinion becomes easier. So even if the delivery or payment mechanisms for broadcasting change, this underlying need for cultural binding will surely survive. There are two responses. One is to try to hold back fragmentation by limiting the supply of new media; a response which would be both futile and damaging. The other is to use the new media opportunities to migrate the virtues of traditional PSB into the digital age. This is the task for current policy makers and the immediate decision is how important a role to assign to the institution of the BBC.

If I am correct about the importance of cultural binding, then the public policy choice at the moment is asymmetric. If we listened to those who wish to restrict the BBC to becoming a limited provider of minority interest content, we would risk destroying the virtues of an institution which can play a vital role in preserving a common culture of tolerance and debate, and one which can implicitly transmit the values of British society to all parts of our society and around the rest of the world. In return we would have to hope that the market would provide the same outcome, despite evidence from other societies that this is not the case. Surely this risk/reward ratio points us in the direction of changing the BBC so it can flourish amid new technologies.

For the moment, the conclusion flows that something as recognisable as the BBC should survive at least until we are on the other side of digital switchover in the middle of the next decade. By then we may be able to see the outlines of a

16 Ofcom (2004b).

different solution to the need for universally available high-quality British content which reaches all parts of our society. Alternatively, we may be able to see how a different method of funding is inescapable, even if we wish to preserve an institution recognisable as the BBC.

At that point, and as long as we maintain the requirement that there is more than one provider of PSB, Government and the public can take a view about the best way to deliver it. In the interim the BBC will need to be more strictly regulated than ever before to ensure that it does not exploit its position in anti-competitive ways. But for those who wish to preserve intelligent democratic debate, who wish Britain to have a distinctive voice which is heard in every corner of the United Kingdom and respected around the world, and who wish that our popular culture remains both peculiarly British and instantly accessible by every Briton, the prospect of deliberately diminishing the role of the BBC will seem absurd. Like many long-lasting and large institutions it is at times irrational, self-important, inward-looking and arrogant. But many other countries around the world wish they had something like it. Britain would be mad to dispense with it.

References

BBC (2004) *Building public value – Renewing the BBC for a digital world*. BBC.

BBC/Human Capital (2004) *Measuring the Value of the BBC – A report by the BBC and Human Capital*. BBC

Brookes, M. (2004) *Watching Alone – Social capital and public service broadcasting*. The Work Foundation in partnership with the BBC.

Fukuyama, F. (1999) *The Great Disruption – Human nature and the Reconstitution of Social Order*. Free Press.

Gray J. (1993) 'Cultural Diversity, National Identity and the Case for Public Service Broadcasting in Britain', in W. Stevenson (ed.) *All our Futures*. London: BFI Publishing.

Ofcom (2004a), *Ofcom Review of Public Service Television Broadcasting: Phase 1 – Is Television Special?*, Office of Communications.

Ofcom (2004b), Ofcom *Review of Public Service Television Broadcasting: Phase 2 – Meeting the Digital Challenge?* Office of Communications.

Putnam, R. D. (2000) *Bowling Alone: The Collapse and Revival of American Community*. New York: Simon & Schuster.

3

The UK's Public Service Broadcasting Ecology

Mark Oliver[1]

---

1. Introduction

When I was Head of Strategy at the BBC in the early 1990s, whenever someone was excited by the large audience share generated by a new programme or strand I would always begin with one question – what was showing on the other side?

Of course time has moved on, and over half of UK households now have access to between 30 and 200 'other sides', but with over 70 per cent of the peak time audience still being taken by the main five channels even in these homes, it is still a relevant question. Between 6pm and 11pm people's viewing habits are in the main initially determined in peak time by a simple choice of which of the five main channels they decide to watch.[2]

This essay begins by setting out to show how questions about the appropriate nature, level and sustainability of public service programming on the UK's

---

1   The analysis in this essay draws upon two previously published reports by Oliver & Ohlbaum Associates. *UK Television Content in the Digital Age*, a report published by the BBC in 2003. *An Initial Analysis of the Issues Raised by Ofcom's Propositions Covering the Public Funding of Currently Commercially Funded PSB TV Channels and Programmes* – a submission to Ofcom's PSTB Phase 1 Review.

2   In reality some individual high profile strands on extra thematic channels probably enter into individual's regular peak time choices, but these strands tend to be different for different demographic groups. As Professor Patrick Barwise pointed out in his *Independent Review of the BBC's Digital Television Services 2004*, the leading channels not only have the highest reach but are also consumed in the greatest volume even in multichannel homes.

commercially funded public service networks (ITV1, Channel 4 and Five) cannot be considered in isolation of the scale, scope and funding of the BBC and its main networks, BBC One and BBC Two.

This is particularly true of the commercially funded network's broader public service remit responsibilities – innovation, high quality drama, home grown programming etc – which are to a large extent encouraged and reinforced by the BBC's own output. But also to a lesser extent by more specific obligations such as arts, religion and regional programming, whose audience share and 'opportunity cost' are influenced by the scheduling policy of the BBC.

Within this context, this essay then goes on to review the specific issue of the sustainability of ITV1, Channel 4 and Five's current public service obligations, and perhaps more importantly, their enforceability.

The essay provides analysis to suggest that the prospects for advertising funding network TV are better than some would make out, and that the ability of those companies who own these networks to sustain their public service commitments are still considerable. The problem, if there is one, is one of the enforceability of what Ofcom has called the public service 'compact' with commercial networks, where regulators can no longer rely on the unique and scarce resource of high reach analogue frequency for leverage.

The essay goes on to suggest that while enforceability might be a problem, it is not as great a problem as some have maintained, as Government and regulators still have leverage in the digital age. Furthermore, in the broader areas of public service broadcasting – such as high quality and innovation – the BBC's funding, scope and scale will become even more vital if commercial broadcasters are to be encouraged rather than cudgeled into behaving in the public interest.

Finally, the essay concludes with a warning and an observation.

Spread public funding of the BBC too thinly and it will simply allow the commercial networks to reduce their remaining public service commitments. Competition between the BBC and the leading commercial networks for audiences for high quality and innovative programming is the bulwark of public service television investment in the UK and will remain so.

Redirect public funding directly to commercially funded broadcasters and the overall level of public service provision in the UK is likely to fall significantly.

Creating competition or contestability in the provision of publicly funded public service television will not be a major step forward if it reduces the broad public service competition between publicly funded television and commercially funded public service television that has given the UK the second strongest indigenous TV content sector in the world able to make a significant contribution to promoting public value in the UK.

2. What's on the other side? The ecology of public service broadcasting

It may seem fairly obvious to point out that the main determinant of what a commercial network channel in any national market has to spend to gain every share point is what rival channels spend.

Competition between commercial networks is unlikely to sustain quality and investment in all but the largest of markets

It might be tempting, given this observation, to conclude that the more competitive the commercial market the greater the investment in programming and the higher the quality of the output. Unfortunately, a market with many separately owned commercial channels is likely to see revenue spread thinly, yielding individual channel schedules of relatively cheap and, outside the USA, often imported programming.

A market with fewer commercial channels, or fewer channel owners at least, might have the capacity to invest more and the commercial freedom to be more innovative, but is likely to have less competitive pressure to do so.

In addition, even where competition between commercial channels can be achieved without spreading revenue too thinly – as in very large national markets such as the USA – there is a tendency for advertising funding to create incentives for channels to over serve the mass market and not make provision for different tastes and demographic groups.

Publicly funded channels raise investment levels across the whole sector without fragmenting revenue or creating private monopolies

In many markets, the solution adopted to this problem has been to provide public funding to one group of channels which then provide competition to another group of commercially funded channels. By spending significant amounts of money on high quality home grown programming, the public channels – it is hoped – will encourage the commercial channels to spend more to reach their optimum long run profit maximizing position.[3]

The idea is that rather than public funding 'crowding out' commercial channel

---

3   Or in the case of a commercially funded not for profit channel such as Channel 4 in the UK, it will encourage the channel to spend more to achieve a given share and reach target.

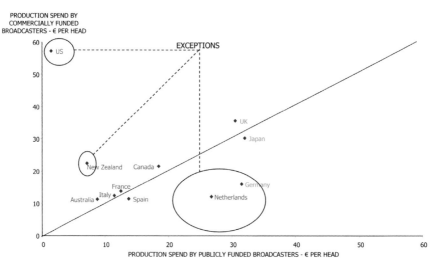

*Figure 1. Production spend per head by publicly funded and commercially funded broadcasters –
2002.*

investment in programming – which might happen if commercial channels were
given public subsidy directly – the existence of well funded public networks
actually has a 'multiplier' effect on commercial channel investment.

Some evidence for this can be seen in Figure 1. This shows that for a number of
countries such as the UK, Japan, France, Italy and Canada, higher home grown
production spending per head by publicly funded channels is correlated to
higher home grown production spending per head on commercial networks.

The exceptions to this trend are relatively easy to explain. In New Zealand,
where public funding is focused on programming rather than channels, it
delivers little positive impact on commercial channel investment in
programming. In fact, it might be argued that some crowding out takes place[+].
In the USA, publicly funded channels are marginal, but conversely, given the size
of the domestic market, their commercial channels are uniquely placed to be
able to afford high budget home grown programming.

In Germany, the public channel system is dominated by the ARD regional
network, which replicates a number of costs including programming spend
across a series of regional broadcasters.[5] In the Netherlands, the public networks

+   This effect is dealt with in Section 6.
5   This is not the same as the ITV network in the UK. ITV has a largely shared peak time schedule to which
each licensee has to contribute. ARD is a much more federal structure with regional station autonomy.

are run on an almost unique pluralist model, where different interest groups have nominated programming slots on each channel.

Both these systems are designed to achieve significant alternative public service purposes, no less legitimate in their national context, than that of increasing the quality and amount of home grown programming, and thereby encouraging the commercial sector to follow suit.

It is interesting to note here that the recent[6] study commissioned as part of Ofcom's *PSTB Phase 2 Review* from McKinsey & Co entitled *Review of Public Service Broadcasting Around the World* found no correlation between the level of public funding and the proportion of hours of domestic programme output on all networks and therefore concluded public investment had no proven positive impact on overall levels of domestic programming in individual markets.

The McKinsey study unfortunately used hours rather than total domestic programme investment and so equated a commercial channel showing endless home grown soaps and quizzes with one investing in new drama series and comedy. It also failed to recognize the specific features of markets such as Germany and the Netherlands that make them atypical.[7]

Publicly funded channels can also help raise standards within more specific public service obligations

Of course, Germany and Netherlands are not the only countries to have other more specific public service goals over and above increasing the level, quality and innovative nature of home grown programming – they simply represent more extreme examples of more specific public service requirements in many markets. As Figure 2 shows, all three commercial public service networks in the UK have both broad requirements on quality, innovation and domestic material and specific requirements for regional programming, arts, news, current affairs and religion.

But even in these more specific areas, it could be argued that having competitive provision by both publicly funded and commercially funded networks improves the overall quality and relevance of the output.

Having established that there might well be a positive link between investment

6   30 September 2004.

7   There are other reasons why Germany and the Netherlands are atypical. Both have a large number of commercial networks, and in both cases the public service broadcasters tend to be less entertainment orientated than in other countries – perhaps lessening the positive competitive pressure on the commercial channels.

	ITV1	CHANNEL 4	FIVE
SPECIAL GENRES	• Peak live news • Religion and arts • Regional news and other • Children's	• News • Current affairs • Religion • Education, social action	• News slot • Current affairs • Religion • Docs and children's
REMIT	• Range of tastes and interests	• Those not catered for by ITV • Ethnic minorities	• Different tone to ITV and C4
NEW PROGRAMME HOURS	• 65% origination	• 60% origination • 40% repeats	• 55% origination • 40% repeats
QUALITY	• Quality drama • Quality entertainment • Quality information		• Quality entertainment and information
OTHER		• Innovative • Experimental	

Figure 2. Public service obligations of commercial networks in the UK.

levels in public channels and those in rival commercial channels, it may be possible to go a stage further and suggest that the greater the overlap between the demographics and general remits of individual publicly funded and commercial funded channels, the greater the multiplier effect of one on the other.

The fact that BBC One's target audience and remit is at least close to ITV1's helps to ensure the maximum competitive interdependence. The same is true of the overlap between Channel 4 and BBC Two. Conversely, if a publicly funded channel's focus differs too markedly from that of a specific rival commercial channel then its impact might well be less.

3. Are the UK's commercial networks in trouble?

There are two levels to any assessment as to whether the UK's commercial networks can sustain their commitment to public service broadcasting in the UK. The first concerns the overall competitive pressures in the commercial market place in the digital age, and whether they cause such a high degree of fragmentation of revenue that both broad commitments to quality and investment and specific commitments to public purpose programming, such as current affairs, come under irresistible pressure.

The second concerns the specific opportunity costs of individual commitments in terms of how much lower costs could be, and how much higher revenue could be, if each obligation were removed.

Set out below is a set of analyses that suggests both the general pressures on the commercial networks and the opportunity costs of their specific requirements might not be as significant as they may first appear.

It is easy to become alarmed about the prospects for commercial networks in the digital age

It is fairly easy to paint a bleak picture for public service commercially funded networks and their ability to support public service obligations in the digital age – superficially the maths is quite compelling. The bleak outlook is based on three factors.

First, thematic channels already take almost 50 per cent share in cable and satellite homes, and almost 25 per cent of all viewing. Once multi-channel TV is available to all, these channels are likely to increase their share significantly, thereby reducing network share substantially.

Second, commercial networks' reliance on advertising makes them particularly vulnerable to audience fragmentation. Not only do they not have recourse to the growing levels of pay TV income in the UK market, but the very future of spot advertising breaks may be threatened by the growth of digital personal video recorders (PVRs) which allow people to fast forward through the advertising breaks.

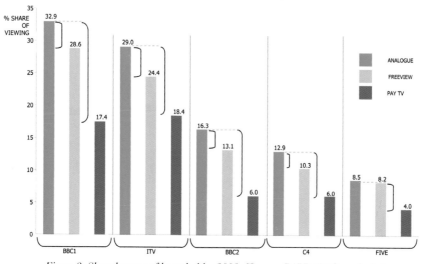

Figure 3. Share by type of household – 2003. [Source: BARB, O&O analysis.]

Even if the future for spot advertising is not quite as bad as this may suggest, it is possible to believe that the networks' current advertising price premium which they enjoy due to their unique high reach, is bound to disappear as they lose share and reach.

Third, while revenue could well decline, the fixed cost nature of broadcasting and programme production means that there is little scope for cost reduction without diluting public service obligations.

Future share fragmentation may be exaggerated

A deeper understanding of UK television economics plus international evidence would suggest that each of the three factors outlined above is being over-exaggerated.

First, audience share decline is unlikely to be as fast as suggested. The highest growth multi channel platform at the moment is Freeview. In Freeview homes the five main networks obtain 85 per cent of the audience rather than 50 per cent of the audience – and even higher shares at peak time. (Figure 3 shows the relative shares in five channel homes, Freeview homes and pay TV homes in the UK for each of the five main networks).

If half the remaining 45 per cent of households not yet converted to digital become Freeview – or Freesat – homes and the other half become cable or satellite homes, the five network all day share is likely to fall to about 55 per cent, and the peak time share remain well above 60 per cent.

Network advertising revenues may well be quite robust

Second, the threat to advertising in general and more specifically the premium rates networks can sell their advertising for may also be not as great as suggested.

While initial users of PVRs do use them to skip advertising, this may be because early adopters are the most keen to avoid advertising. More importantly, those willing to supply PVR functionality at effectively subsidized prices – the digital TV platform owners – are slowing down the forward wind speed of the equipment to ensure that viewers can see the adverts – even if at high speed.[8]

Even if this still results in some degree of advertising skipping, it is likely that broadcasters will make up some of this revenue through expansion in their

---

8   Research has suggested that viewers' recall of adverts is higher if seen at high speed.

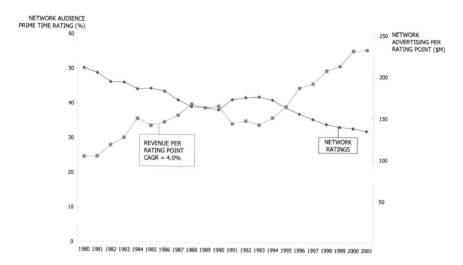

Figure 4. USA network spot advertising revenue per rating point (constant 1980 prices) and network ratings. [Sources: Veronis, Suhler Associates, Wilkofski, Gruen Associates.]

sponsorship inventory, and that more value will simply be placed on the beginning and end slots of an advertising break.

While fragmentation may eventually impact the advertising price premium achieved by networks, all the evidence so far is that this price premium remains, and in fact might even grow. Figure 4 shows what has happened in the USA as network share has fallen rapidly from 1980 to 2001. Figure 5 shows the current pattern of prices, with the leading US networks still being able to charge a higher price than all but the most demographically appealing thematic channels and still gaining far higher peak time share despite multichannel TV being available in 80 per cent of homes.

This trend suggests that as the main commercial networks lose audience impacts to thematic channels their advertising price rises to partially compensate for this loss. This pattern seems to have been repeated so far in the UK – most evidently for ITV and Channel 4 – which both sell at a much higher price than Five. Overall recent trends suggest that for every percentage point share lost by the major networks, price increases by about half a percentage point (Figure 6).

Ofcom's Phase 2 report suggested that ITV's ability to raise the price of its airtime as its audience share fell in the future would be prohibited by the new pricing formula applied to its airtime selling practices as a condition of the merger of Granada and Carlton – the so called Contracts Rights Renewal (CRR)

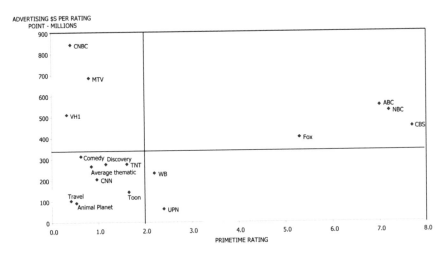

Figure 5. Primetime household rating vs. advertising revenue per rating point of US TV channels – 2001.

formula. This would suggest that in 2004 and beyond, ITV's price will not rise as it loses share.

However, the CRR formula is essentially a way of locking in the discounts to ITV's average station price enjoyed by major advertisers rather than a cap on the station price itself. As ITV's share falls, advertisers that need the relatively high

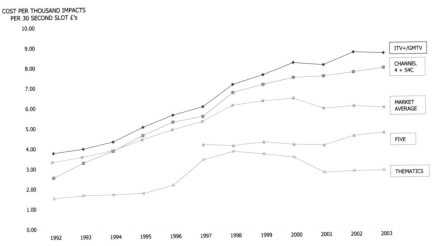

Figure 6. UK TV cost per thousand impacts trend 1992–2003.
[Source: ITC, BSkyB, Bear Stearns, Advertising Association, O&O analysis.]

reach supplied by ITV will want to buy the same number of impacts even though the overall level of impacts ITV can supply falls. This suggests that ITV's average price may well still increase even though major advertisers will be able to claim their existing discounts to that price.

Of course, over time if ITV's share falls dramatically, advertisers might feel they can replace it with a combination of Five and thematic channels. This would imply that ITV's price premium would either not increase or actually fall. But this has little to do with the CRR pricing formula itself. Evidence to date in the UK suggests that ITV's share has not yet fallen sufficiently to erode this price premium, and evidence from the USA suggests that as long as commercial networks maintain higher peak time reach than any rival channels, they can still enjoy a price premium even if their share declines quite markedly.

New opportunities in the digital age are likely to present network owners with the potential to exploit significant economies of scale and scope

One of the biggest threats to the economics of ITV1, Channel 4 and Five may well be the emergence of a new high reach free-to-air network on the back of growing digital distribution, rather than the gradual erosion of their audience by the 200 or so thematic channels in the UK.

But this threat can be countered by the creation of new mini networks by ITV, Channel 4 and Five which effectively help protect their overall share of audience and when combined with the main channel help to sustain high reach.[9] The commercial networks' leading position – even in cable and satellite homes – means they are in prime position to exploit these economies of scale and scope in the digital age, thus helping to preserve their overall financial health.

Similarly, the digital age is likely to provide more and more opportunities for the secondary exploitation of programming in the UK and overseas. This in turn should mean that commercial network broadcasters should, other things being equal, be able either to pay less for the primary use of any commissioned programme from independent suppliers or benefit from the secondary exploitation of their in-house programming.

While the UK market is very unlikely to move towards the levels of so called deficit financing of new programmes experienced in the USA – where often only 75 to 80 per cent of a programme's costs are met by the first network commission – some reduction of commission costs is possible.

---

9   ITV already has ITV2 and ITV 3 as effectively extra free-to-air channels and Channel 4 is planning to launch More4.

The USA's large export market, and its large scale use of US library material – rather than imported material – for its thematic channels, means that its own secondary revenues for any given programme are more significant than those for a UK commissioned programme, thus allowing for a greater deficit on initial commission funding. However, overseas earnings of UK producers and distributors have been growing by over 10 per cent a year over the last five years with DVD sales and format deals adding to the traditional sale of ready made programmes. This should allow broadcasters to negotiate tighter prices on first commissions while still leaving producers with healthy margins and return on capital.[10]

Digital is also bringing with it new revenue streams around the broadcast of programmes themselves. Call revenues, interactive advertising and associated interactive gaming and betting are all likely to be available to commercial networks on some or all of their digital distribution platforms.

Overall then, the prospects for ITV1, Channel 4 and Five would appear quite strong in the digital age – at the very least there would seem to be plenty of opportunities to counter the undoubted threats.

4. What are the real opportunity costs of public service obligations?

Opportunity costs have to be seen within the overall context of mixed schedule network broadcasting

Even within generally healthy commercial network broadcasters it might still be the case that some types of public service output represent a significant opportunity cost that is likely to grow as digital switchover proceeds. For an opportunity cost to be present within a commercial network it has to be the case that a channel could make more profit– or a smaller loss – from a realistic alternative schedule.

Before analysing the nature and extent of these opportunity costs it is worth recognising that all mixed schedule network broadcasters earn different margins

---

10 It is very important to stress that any price reductions from commissioning broadcasters would reflect a general market based increase in secondary values – something that has happened in the area of animation already. This is not suggesting that networks should use any market power they have to penalise the producer of a commercially valuable programme by effectively 'netting off' the specific secondary revenue potential of that programme from the commission price paid. Such so called 'netting off' behaviour has been the subject of Ofcom intervention on terms of trade with independent producers and is quite rightly being restricted as it penalises the successful producer.

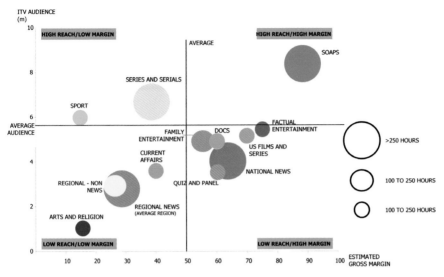

Figure 7. ITV schedule economics, 5pm – 11pm, 2003.

from different types of programming. Figure 7 above sets out the estimated gross margin by programme genre for ITV in 2003.

This shows that while ITV's average gross margin – advertising less programme costs – is around 50 per cent, this varies from 15 per cent for arts and religion to over 80 per cent for soaps. It also shows fairly strong margins on news and current affairs although the audiences are relatively low. Margins on drama series are also quite low, but apart from soaps and major sporting events this type of programming is the only genre to consistently generate high audiences.

One might be tempted to conclude from this analysis that an ITV drama series imposes an opportunity cost on ITV – if it could replace them with soaps and factual entertainment it might be able to achieve some high audiences and improve margins. However, this is unlikely to be the case as marginal audience rating returns to extra soap hours or factual entertainment might be much lower than for a drama series. At the extreme, an all soap channel would be unlikely to get a share similar to ITV's.

Similar observations might be made of Channel 4's schedule set out in Figure 8 below. One might conclude that Channel 4 should drop news and drama from its schedule as the opportunity costs are very high – but would Channel 4 be as popular overall if it had no news or home grown drama series? One might also conclude that swapping its news for factual entertainment or imported TV series and film might significantly improve the channel's financial position, but there

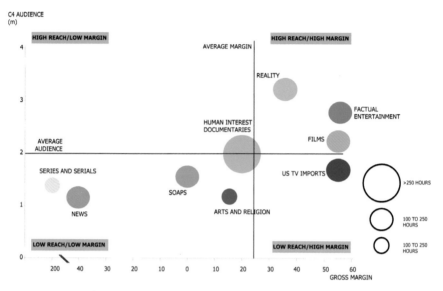

Figure 8. Channel 4 schedule economics, 5pm – 11pm, 2003.

is no guarantee that if Channel 4 replaced its 200 hours of news with factual entertainment it would generate anywhere near the average audience and margins that are achieved by its current output of factual entertainment, nor that the schedules of BBC Two and Five would not change should such a strategy be adopted.

Opportunity costs – a lesson from history

Perhaps the best example ever of how care must be taken over calculating opportunity costs was the move of ITV's main late evening news bulletin from 10pm to 11pm and then back to 10.30 pm.

ITV had calculated that they could gain greater audience share by moving their news to 11pm giving them the chance to run dramas and films from 9pm to 11pm uninterrupted. They therefore convinced the Independent Television Commission (ITC) to let them move their news bulletin to 11pm on the grounds this would make them financially stronger and able to maintain both more investment in news but also other areas of public service programming.

Unfortunately, these calculations, while probably correct in themselves, had not factored in the possibility that if the ITV news moved to 11pm, the BBC might find the best way to maximize its news audience – a legitimate goal for a public service institution – was to move it to 10pm. In due course this happened, putting ITV's 9pm to 10pm audience share under pressure – as the BBC could for the first time run major dramas and features from 9pm to 10pm – and leaving ITV's 11pm news audience in the doldrums.

The opportunity cost of the 10pm news on ITV had been wrongly specified by not factoring in the optimal response from the other main broadcaster.[11]

Opportunity costs have to be calculated with reference to real alternatives

So when reviewing the various margins for ITV and Channel 4 on different genres, calculating the opportunity cost is not simply about replacing low margin genres or strands with higher margin genres or strands, or even about replacing low margin genres with the average channel margin. A full calculation of opportunity cost has to be compared with the most likely outcome of any change given the responses all other channels – the BBC, other commercial networks – and, probably to a lesser extent, thematic channels.

The opportunity costs to ITV of having regional news, arts and documentaries are not simply about the fact that they currently earn them lower margins than average. If ITV were to abandon its regional news programmes at 6pm, there is no guarantee that Channel 4 would keep *The Simpsons* on in that slot, nor that the BBC would necessarily keep its national news at 6pm. The overall impact of the change could well be to hand all the regional news audience to the BBC, while ITV had to slog it out with popular entertainment programming on Channel 4 and Five. Just as with the *News at 10* move, the opportunity costs could well be much lower than they appear through a simple comparison of today's relative margins.

5. Is the problem more a question of enforceability – the public service 'compact'

Are the opportunity costs of obligations becoming greater than the privileges of being a public service commercial broadcaster?

Even if opportunity costs are lower than have been estimated by Ofcom at £260m for ITV and £160m for Channel 4, there is still a concern that the benefits gained by commercial networks from having privileged access to scarce analogue spectrum will reduce as digital switchover approaches, while the opportunity costs of public service obligations increase. This may be particularly

11 This is in fact a classic lesson of game theory – i.e. to factor in the potential response of competitors to tease out the likely new equilibrium once each party decides on their best strategy given the likely options of the other.

the case with ITV and Five[12] who currently pay a fee for their analogue spectrum access.

It is feared that as the proportion of analogue only households declines the benefits of analogue spectrum will be less than the extra opportunity costs of their obligations (even if lower than estimated), giving these channels a strong incentive to hand their analogue licences back.

Ofcom has estimated that the total value of the privileges offered to commercial PSB channels within digital only transmissions will amount to just £25m a year per channel. This is based primarily on a valuation of their privileged access to digital terrestrial spectrum, their prime placement on digital electronic programme guides (EPGs), and their must-carry status on cable and satellite systems.

The relatively low value placed on a prime EPG listing slot is based on analysis of the impact on the audience share of BBC Three and BBC Four when they moved up the listings – which was seen to be marginal. However, the impact on Channel 4, for instance, of losing its place as the fourth position on the EPG to say, Sky One, and perhaps being relegated to the second page of the EPG would probably be much more significant than suggested by the Ofcom analysis, especially when analogue broadcasting ceased.

Similarly, the must-carry status on cable and satellite relates to the value of the current rules on carriage which while stating that these services must be carried on cable and satellite systems allow satellite operators to levy relatively high charges for encryption.[13]

A stronger must-carry obligation which allowed for encryption at incremental costs only might be of far more value, although it would represent an imposition on Sky.

Gaining extra spectrum on the highest reach digital multiplexes may well make the difference between being able to establish a new mini-network to protect the main channel's position and seeing that position lost to a rival.

---

12 As the only shareholder in Channel 4, the Government does have the enforcement mechanism of ending its zero dividend policy with the channel.

13 Even though public service commercial networks are free-to-air, they need to be encrypted on satellite systems to prevent unauthorized reception outside the UK. If they are not encrypted – as is the case currently with the BBC, they are likely to incur higher rights fees from sports bodies and film studios, as well as higher transmission charges (as they have to broadcast each regional opt out on a separate feed).

Are there other ways of enforcing or encouraging the public service compact short of providing public funding?

Even if the direct privileges of access and distribution to viewers do decline over time and are eventually less than the opportunity costs of public service broadcasting, there may be other broader privileges that can be bestowed upon commercially funded public service broadcasters.

In the case of Channel 4, the waiving of any dividend requirement by Government is a significant privilege that might be reversed if Channel 4 decided to unilaterally drop its public service obligations. In the case of ITV, the green light given to consolidation despite the channels more than 50 per cent share of the UK TV advertising market and its clear ability to charge more than the market average price, was in part given in order to help ITV sustain its public service requirements and provide effective competition to the BBC in the digital age.

Looking forward, a greater degree of consolidation could be allowed for public service networks than purely commercial ones, allowing them an enhanced ability to exploit economies of scale and scope than their purely commercial rivals.

6. Re-directing public funding – issues and concerns

If commercial network sustainability is seriously threatened, and if the opportunity costs of their specific public service obligations end up being higher than the privileges, then, and only then, it may be worth considering the use of public funds to help provide their public service obligations. This can be in the form of providing public funding for specific programmes, annual grants in aid to specific channels or simply the facility to cover an out-turn loss with a subsidy.

But there are several problems associated with such moves, many of which have been recognized in Ofcom's PSB review Phase 2 report.

Allocating a proportion of public funding to commercial channels or programmes on commercial channels risks a significant crowding out effect

In a fragmenting TV environment it may well be superficially attractive to reduce the financial burden on commercial channels of public service obligations by offering to part fund them from public funds. It may also seem a very effective way of securing greater reach for specific areas of public service programming by placing and funding such programming across a range of otherwise commercial channels and schedules. Lastly, by getting rival channels to 'contest' for this public funding it seems to ensure that the most cost effective propositions succeed.

However, while public funding of commercial channel public service broadcasting might offer the potential to reach more viewers with such programming more cost effectively, it raises significant incentive and 'gatekeeper' problems that are likely to mean that potential is never realized.

While providing public funds to commercial broadcasters or programmes might promise to improve the reach of public service outputs, this can be countered by the reduced effectiveness of the funded programming in promoting public service objectives

Public funding does not remove the essential conflict between the objectives of a commercially funded broadcaster and the objectives of those providing the funds.

Where the broadcasters are profit maximising, as with ITV and Five, there will always be a tendency for the broadcasters to either move funded programming out of the better slots, or dilute the public service component of any given programme type once funded. This incentive incompatibility between the 'gatekeeper' and those providing the public funding may well prevent the achievement of the public service goals of any fund.[14]

Furthermore, any method which tops-up commercial funding for programmes with public funding runs a very real risk of simply crowding out investment that would have been made by the commercial sector.

Commercially funded broadcasters have every incentive to exaggerate the need for public subsidy so they can divert their own funding to maximise their own objectives. In the case of ITV and Five that objective is maximising profits, in the case of Channel 4 that objective might be maximising surpluses for investment in other ventures, as has been the case in the past.

These dilution and crowding out effects are even more likely if public service television is defined in terms of the purposes or characteristics of a programme type – as Ofcom seems to favour – rather than limited to certain pre-specified genres. Those allocating public funds will never quite know if the specific subject or format would have been funded commercially in any case.

In order to limit the level of crowding out that occurs, or the ability of commercial broadcasters to use their 'gatekeeper' role to limit the effectiveness

---

14 Ofcom's *PSTB Phase 1 Review* has already drawn attention to the recent trend for ITV to move its current commitments out of peak time schedules – programme funding does not change this incentive.

of any public funding, any scheme that allows commercial channels to access public finance actually needs to have stricter rules than currently on either public service output hours requirements, or actual channel spending levels and/or the use of channel surpluses.

Funds going to programmes on ITV would have to be safeguarded by either scheduling guarantees or minimum spending commitments, in order to ensure ITV was not simply using public funds to subsidise shareholders. Funds going to Channel 4 might also have to be accompanied by minimum spending commitments across the whole channel schedule and limitations on the use of core channel surpluses, thereby helping to prevent any future potential large scale recycling of public funds into commercial ventures.

This implies that public funding for public service on commercially funded channels does not solve any problems of enforceability – it may make them even worse.

Allocating the public funds to one or more channels as an annual grant in aid – while it might have lower running costs than a fund which financed individual programmes – would not avoid these problems of crowding out or the need for very strict output requirements to ensure that the public investment was really additional to commercial spending.

Reducing BBC funding to subsidise commercial channels risks a double crowding out effect

Section 2 laid out how the funding levels of publicly funded broadcasters might well be expected to determine the spending needed by commercial rivals. In essence, they reduce the opportunity cost for a commercial channel of spending on, for example, drama, comedy and documentaries to almost zero, as there are no other more profitable alternatives given what is on the other side.

Ofcom's own modeling of the commercial sector's prospects in the digital age recognizes the link between the overall spending and investment in the BBC, and the spending and investment by ITV1, Channel 4 and Five. The model is driven by the link between any network's share of overall market programme spend and its share of audience, and then the link between the share of audience and its revenue. If the BBC invests more in BBC One, then ITV1 will lose share both to the BBC but also in relative terms to Channel 4 and Five and, therefore, lose revenue.

While ITV could simply accept this share and revenue loss, it may well be better off spending extra money as well in order to regain share and revenue. ITV's decision rests on its ability to generate incremental audience from incremental spend – its so called incremental 'efficiency ratio'. The same calculations apply in slightly different contexts to Channel 4 and Five.

Given that all the commercial channels have increased their programming budgets over the last five years (Ofcom's own analysis suggests this has been at between 4.7 and 8 per cent a year) in reaction to similar rates of increase at the BBC, it would seem that the commercial channels are still opting to spend more on programming as their preferred strategy given the competitive dynamics of the UK market. A significant factor in this decision – given the direct rivalries – must be the level of funding commitment at the BBC.

In such circumstances, any switch of the money from the BBC to funding programming on commercial channels is likely to cause a cycle of decline in quality and innovation. The commercial channels may be given the money to provide public service programming, but the main competitive pressure to actually provide it – especially in important dimensions such as quality and innovation – has been reduced.

More generally, having a well funded BBC, may actually raise the minimum costs needed to establish a relatively high reach, high share channel. This in turn protects ITV, Channel 4 and Five from further revenue fragmenting market entry.

Switching money from the BBC to commercially funded channels, therefore, not only runs the normal crowding out risks from providing public funding to commercial organisations, but also reduces the external pressures on those commercial channels to maintain their current levels of investment and the commitment to quality and innovative programming.

This implies a double crowding out impact, where commercial channels can afford to significantly reduce their investment levels to fund either new ventures or returns to shareholders.

Splitting public funding between rival publicly funded bodies runs the risk of reducing any multiplier effect

An alternative to giving public monies to commercial channels to make up for any shortfall in public service provision would be to increase the funding and scope of publicly funded broadcasters.

An alternative way of achieving this than simply increasing the funding of the BBC, could be to set up a new publicly funded provider, as has been suggested in Ofcom's *PSTB Phase 2 Review*.

If this new organisation's ambitions were just to provide the public service obligations that were no longer enforceable or sustainable on ITV, Channel 4 and Five – i.e. only additional commitments to that being provided by the BBC and still being provided by ITV, Channel 4 and Five[15] – then it could avoid the crowding out concerns associated with public funding of commercial channels.

However, if this new public service institution started to draw funds away from the BBC to provide a greater share of the overall public service provision in the UK, it would be likely to reduce the competitive pressure on the commercial networks to increase investment in high quality and innovative home grown programming.

Taking monies out of BBC One and BBC Two and redistributing them to a new institution less focused on healthy rivalry with ITV, Channel 4 or Five, would in effect allow the commercial networks to reduce their remaining public service commitments by reducing the multiplier effect the BBC has on the commercial sector.

Rather than being the solution to a reducing public service provision on commercial channels the new institution could well become the cause of that reduction. In effect crowding out of commercial channel investment would still take place.

---

15 ITV, for instance, would still presumably be providing a large quantity of high cost home grown drama as this is likely to remain sustainable and would be the only way for it to compete with a properly funded BBC.

4

Measuring the Value Created by the BBC

Simon Terrington and Caroline Dollar

Introduction

This essay is based on the findings of a research survey carried out by the BBC and Human Capital between December 2003 and May 2004.[1] The study represents the first ever large-scale attempt to quantify the total value that the BBC is perceived to generate, not only as a service to individuals as consumers, but also to the population as a whole.

The unique public service obligations attached to the BBC mean that it is required to deliver value to the UK population both as consumers and as citizens. This means that across its broadcast, online and digital activity it is expected to satisfy the immediate viewing needs of individual households (consumer value) as well as creating a halo of educational, cultural, democratic and social benefits to the population as a whole (citizen value). The consumer value and the citizen value together make up the total value produced by the BBC.

The valuation of public services is an area of growing interest. Comparable studies have been carried out on the The British Library and the Danish National Theatre. Research into broadcaster value has been conducted on CBC Canada (2000) and RTÉ Ireland (2003).

---

1 The full methodology and research findings can be found in *Measuring the Value of the BBC – A report by the BBC and Human Capital*, 2004.

Previous work on the BBC itself has tended to focus on its consumer value rather than its total value. Research carried out by the Home Office in 1987, for example, explored potential subscription prices for a package of BBC One and BBC Two.[2] Similarly, in the London Business School's 1990 study, Ehrenberg and Mills explored potential price points for packages of BBC One and/or BBC Two.[3] Both reports recommended against subscription due to the loss of revenue and audience numbers, as well as the high administration costs that it would entail. These studies looked at what people were prepared to pay for the BBC rather than what they thought it was worth. Also the research was carried out too early to incorporate the effect of advances in digital television.

In 2000 the Radiocommunications Agency investigated potential subscription charges for a package of all five terrestrial channels and for a package of satellite channels.[4] This went some way towards valuing the BBC against the developing multichannel backdrop, but it did not arrive at individual values for its constituent services.

The most recent investigation into the value created by public service broadcasters, including the BBC, was carried out by Ofcom as part of its PSTB review.[5] They used deliberative research to explore attitudes across the population to a number of potential funding scenarios for public service broadcasting. They did not attempt to place a number on the value generated by the BBC.

Methodology

The BBC's consumer value represents the amount that people would be willing to pay for the BBC as a subscription service. We used the Gabor-Granger technique to investigate the consumer value and to identify the price at which the BBC would maximise its revenue as a subscription service. This is a well-used method, commonly employed to gauge the optimal price points for consumer products.

The consumer value is inadequate, however, as a means of understanding how much the BBC is worth to the population as a whole. Willingness to pay is, to a great extent, dependent on the affluence of the respondents. This can be illustrated with an example. Take two children, A and B. A comes from a rich

---

2   *Subscription Television: A Study for the Home Office*, 1987.

3   Andrew Ehrenberg and Pam Mills, *Viewers' Willingness to Pay*, London Business School, 1990.

4   *Survey to determine the consumers' surplus accruing to TV viewers and radio listeners*, Radiocommunications Agency (DTI), 2000.

5   *Ofcom Public Service Broadcasting Review: Phase 2 Meeting the Digital Challenge*, 2004.

family and spends every holiday abroad. B comes from a less wealthy family and has never been abroad. If offered a trip to France, child B might be willing to pay less than child A but would probably value it more. If a profit-maximising broadcaster was offering the trip then it would take child A. If the BBC was offering the trip then it would take child B as a priority, although it would hopefully take child A as well. As the BBC is funded by a regressive tax, its value should not be gauged by a metric which puts more weight on the preferences of the most affluent. It is simply not appropriate to incentivise the BBC to focus on delivering value to the wealthiest members of society. If willingness to pay was the sole metric by which the success of the BBC was measured, it would end up behaving little differently to a commercial broadcaster such as Sky. The BBC's public service remit means that it creates externalities and merit goods which are not included within the consumer value.

In order to capture these externalities and merit goods we also investigated the total value generated by the BBC for society as a whole. Finding out what people think the BBC is worth (instead of what they are willing to pay) helps to reduce the impact of affluence on the overall equation. Resources are allocated to public service by the democratic process (rather than the market) and any changes to its current funding structure would be decided by an elected and accountable government. Accordingly, we designed a question which would relate to respondents as voting citizens or democratic agents.

At first we considered asking people how they would feel if the government decided to turn the BBC into a subscription service. We were worried, however, that respondents might end up confusing the licence fee with other front-of-mind policy issues. Therefore we devised a question which simulated a national referendum. We asked people to vote either for the total closure of the BBC or for its continuation at a range of prices, from which the respondent was free to choose. In this way the respondent was asked to think on behalf of the country as a whole and to consider the BBC as an all-or-nothing option, which would disappear altogether if he or she chose not to pay.

Using these two methods (Gabor-Granger and our 'national voting' question) we arrived at the BBC's value to consumers as well as its value to society as a whole. Our methodology does have two key limitations which should be highlighted at this point. Firstly, when people answer as consumers they inevitably factor in some externalities. One can draw a parallel here with consumers buying 'green' products. The Body Shop, for example, makes prominent use of its animal-friendly manufacturing methods in its marketing and advertising. When people buy cosmetics from The Body Shop, they may be acting as good citizens who want to benefit society as a whole. It is equally probable that they are buying the cosmetics because they derive self-satisfaction or consumer value from their purchase.

Differentiating consumer welfare and citizen welfare is a task that will never be completely accurate. Our qualitative research revealed that when valuing the BBC, the respondents who were addressed as consumers thought primarily about the programmes that they usually watch and enjoy but that they also thought about genres like news, which they knew they ought to be watching. This means that some of the BBC's citizen value may be buried within what we report to be the consumer value. We are likely to have overestimated the consumer value and to have therefore underestimated the citizen value.

A second limitation of our research is that when people were asked about the value created by the BBC for society as a whole they responded with their *perceptions* of the value created by its externalities. This is, of course, quite different to the *real* value of the externalities. It could, in fact, be argued that consumer research is incapable of ever arriving at an accurate measurement of the value created by the BBC. The very nature of merit goods means that their value can only ever be known in the future.

The blurring of consumer and citizen value, as well as actual and perceived externalities, means that our research can only ever represent an approximation of the BBC's value. We found the consumer/ total value split to be a helpful filter through which to analyse the BBC. In addition, it enabled us to compare the value generated by the licence fee with the amount that would be created through a subscription system. By subtracting the consumer value from the total value we believe we have arrived at some idea of the citizen value. It is impossible to ignore, however, that the citizen value is, to a great extent, dependent on the consumer value. In almost every interaction the two are intertwined. It is virtually impossible to imagine a transaction that delivered only value to citizens. This overlap is illustrated most effectively by the genre-ranking test which is discussed later in this essay.

Results

Our study was carried out on a nationally representative sample of 2,257 respondents. Half of the respondents were asked to think as consumers about how much they would be willing to pay for the BBC as a subscription service. The remaining half were addressed as citizens and were asked about how much the BBC and its individual services are worth to the population as a whole. The

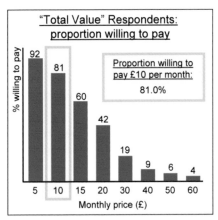

Figure 1.

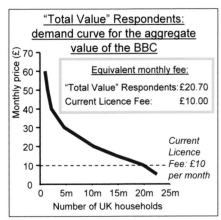

Figure 2.

robustness of the methodology was checked over the course of several pilots and an additional qualitative study was used to refine the questionnaire wording.

The research revealed that the population as a whole are overwhelmingly in favour of the licence fee. 81 per cent of the UK population believe it is worth its current annual rate of £121 and around half of the respondents said that the BBC was worth at least £20.70 per month or twice its current cost (see Figures 1 and 2 above). There appears to be strong democratic backing for the BBC.

It is revealing to consider the value people perceive the BBC to deliver in terms of the net citizen surplus. That is the difference between the total amount of value which the BBC is perceived to deliver to the entire population and the total amount of revenue collected through the licence fee. According to this study the BBC currently delivers a surplus of £3.3bn to citizens of the UK in return for the licence fee (see Figure 3 below).

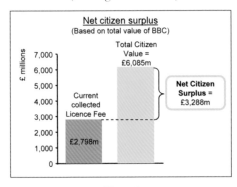

Figure 3.

When each of the BBC's constituent services are examined more closely, BBC One is given the highest value by all respondents, at between £5 and £6 per month, or half the existing monthly licence fee. As you would expect, this is followed by BBC Two. The sum of the perceived value of these two services alone almost totals the current £10 monthly licence fee.

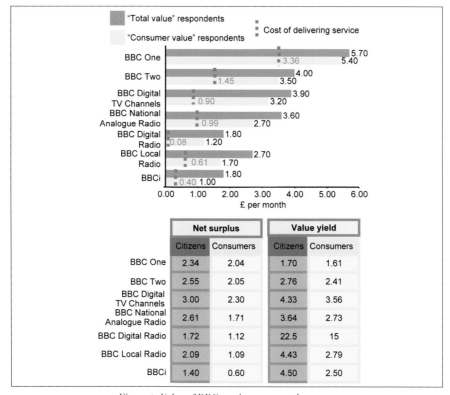

Figure 4. Value of BBC services compared to costs.

The digital channels are valued relatively highly at between £3 and £4 per month. BBCi is allocated the lowest value at between £1 and £2. Overall, every single one of the BBC's services is considered to deliver value far in excess of its cost (see Figure 4).[6] This net surplus is similar for each of its seven services although it is worth noting that both digital television and digital radio fare particularly well in this analysis. When the net surplus for each service is expressed relative to its cost, as a value yield, the digital channels which operate from a very low cost base are shown to generate exceptionally good value for money. This is particularly the case for digital radio.

Our analysis also calculated the net surplus generated by each of the digital television channels. When the channels are examined individually BBC News 24, CBBC and CBeebies deliver the highest value yields (see Figure 5). This gives

6   Prompting in this question means that the aggregate value of the BBC (when calculated as the sum of the values of the individual services) is slightly higher than in the question about the value of the entire BBC.

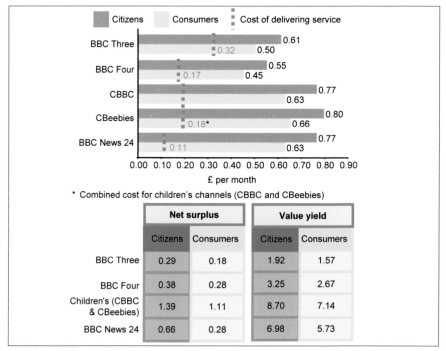

Figure 5. BBC digital channels and radio stations individual service values compared to costs.

every indication that the BBC's digital channels play a significant role in the creation of consumer welfare.

Unsurprisingly, the digital channels tend to receive the highest values from respondents in multichannel homes. It is fascinating, though, that they are still valued highly by those living in analogue households who are likely to have less awareness or knowledge of them. Our qualitative research revealed that, despite their unfamiliarity with these channels, analogue respondents believed them to operate at a similar level of quality as the BBC's terrestrial channels. Consequently they awarded them with unexpectedly high values.

People from multichannel homes award the highest values to the BBC throughout our study. Whilst multichannel has reduced people's overall consumption of BBC television, this has not caused people to stop appreciating its value. In fact multichannel has in some ways set a high benchmark for the cost of the BBC. Young, wealthy men who are spending as much as £30–£40 per month on movie and live sport packages are now used to high subscription charges and therefore place some of the highest values on the BBC. They are prominent in the 6 per cent of our sample who said the BBC was worth £50 a month, or five times the current licence fee.

Young people are similarly enthusiastic about the value of the BBC. 16–29 year olds, on average, estimate the monthly total value of the BBC to be £22.68, where the average response is £20.70. They particularly value digital TV (especially BBC Three), digital radio and BBCi. Many of them are living at home where the licence fee is paid by their parents. For this reason, their answers tend not to be anchored to its current cost in the same way as those of the older respondents. Assuming they continue to hold these views, this bodes well for generations to come.

So far we have looked at the 81 per cent of the population who believe the BBC to be worth its current price. Let us now consider the dissatisfied 19 per cent who remain. In 1990, Ehrenberg and Mills found a similar group of the population who were unwilling to pay £72 a year as the licence fee was then set for BBC One and Two. At that time the group comprised only 10 per cent of the population. The advent of multichannel television is the most likely explanation for this group having virtually doubled in size.

Our group can be divided into two parts. Firstly, the 'non-payers' or 11 per cent of the population who are willing to pay for the BBC but not at its current rate. They tend to be C2DE families with multichannel television, skewed to Scotland and Northern Ireland. There can be no doubt that the multiplication of available channels has, to some extent, reduced the value these people place on the BBC. However, most interestingly, the qualitative research revealed that many of these people believe they are already paying for the BBC through their multichannel subscription. This group should in no way be viewed as a lost cause. In our view, it is more than likely that they could be won back through a strategic marketing and communications campaign as well as a few well-targeted scheduling decisions.

The second group consists of all-out refuseniks who oppose the very principle of paying anything at all for the BBC. This 8 per cent of the sample consider even £5 a month to be too much. They tend to be older, DE men from Scotland and Northern Ireland. Very few of them have access to multichannel television. The group is of a similar size to the 7 per cent of the population who currently dodge the licence fee. They feel alienated and underserved by the BBC, its products and services. These refuseniks would be much harder to bring back to the BBC than the earlier group of 'non-payers'.

The BBC has tracked approval scores for its services for a long time. We thought

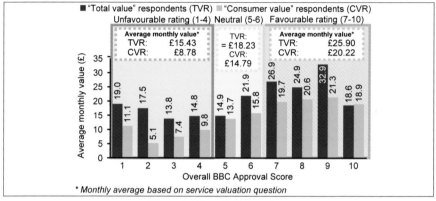

Figure 6. Value of BBC services.

it would be interesting to compare approval scores with perceived value. When we asked respondents to give approval scores to the BBC there was little difference between the scores given by the respondents who were asked to think about consumer value and those who were asked to think about the BBC's total value (see Figure 6). On average, the 'total value' respondents gave slightly higher and slightly less polarised scores than the 'consumer value' respondents, averaging 6.78 compared to 6.95. Reassuringly, when respondents' approval scores are plotted against their valuations of the BBC, there is a direct correlation. The respondents who award the highest approval scores to the BBC tend to value it the most highly (see Figure 7).

When we investigated the motivations behind respondents' approval scores, high quality programming was revealed to be the most important component in

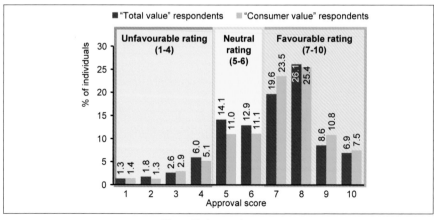

Figure 7. Approval scores.

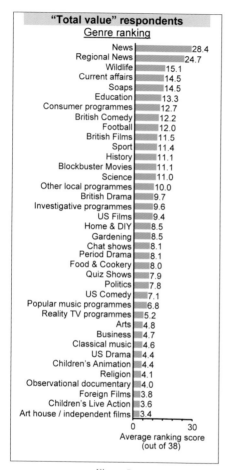

Figure 8.

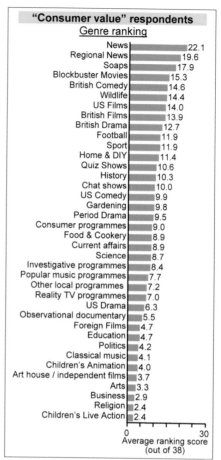

Figure 9.

creating value. 49 per cent of 'total value' respondents and 59 per cent of 'consumer value' respondents linked their approval rating to programme quality, demonstrating the essential role it has to play in people's perceptions of the BBC's value.

In order to understand better the role of programme quality, we explored the contribution made by each of the BBC's broadcast genres to its overall value. The 'total value' respondents were asked about the importance of different genres to the country as a whole, whilst the 'consumer value' respondents were asked about the types of programme they prefer. The former group ranked news, regional news, wildlife, current affairs and soaps the most highly. The latter group chose news, regional news, soaps, blockbuster movies and British

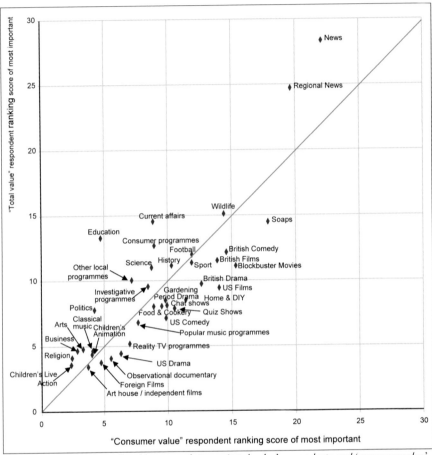

Figure 10. Comparison of ranking scores between 'total value' respondents and 'consumer value' respondents.

comedy. Homegrown genres like British comedy, soaps, drama and British film tended to score highly throughout the sample. Arts and religion tended to be valued less highly. Figures 8 and 9 show the average score received by each genre, out of 38, where a score of 38 would mean that everyone placed that genre as their most important and a score of 0 would mean that everyone placed it as the least important.

When the genre ranking results from both sets of respondents are plotted against one another, the crossover is remarkable (see Figure 10). News and regional news are ranked first and second by both sets of respondents. These results are consistent with the findings in Ofcom's review of public service television broadcasting.[7] The two groups of respondents differ over current affairs which is ranked higher by the 'total value' respondents and blockbuster movies which are valued more by the 'consumer value' respondents. On the whole, however, they are broadly in agreement.

The high correlation between the results from both groups of respondents illustrates the difficulty in separating consumer and citizen value which was outlined earlier in the essay. The results here imply that perceptions of citizen value are not restricted to the traditionally 'worthy' genres. Football and soaps are equally appreciated for their citizen value. Even blockbuster movies are seen as important for the country as a whole. Similarly, the high ranking of news and regional news among 'consumer value' respondents is once against evidence of the way in which consumer value can become infused by citizen value.

Further to ranking the genres in order of importance, we investigated the data to understand how the genres are ranked by different types of people within the audience. This enabled us to explore how genre preferences are linked to perceptions of programme quality and value. Here we used factor analysis in order to uncover the variables which are most likely to determine audience members' preferences. We discovered a clear story in terms of socio-economic groups. ABC1s value the high-brow genres such as arts, music and period dramas, whilst C2DEs enjoy the entertainment genres like soaps, blockbuster movies and reality television.

There is no obvious distinction between genre preferences in different areas of the UK. The English place slightly more value on home-produced television. In Northern Ireland audiences are especially interested in US programming and sport. Religion rates relatively highly among audiences in Wales and Northern Ireland.

In terms of audience members' approval ratings, those who gave a high approval rating to the BBC tend to value politics, current affairs and the high arts. It is difficult to know whether the BBC is particularly good at these areas and so people who like them like the BBC, or indeed whether the kind of people who like the BBC also tend to like these genres. Those who award the lowest approval ratings tend to value US programming and feature films.

Across the age groups, 16–29 year olds place the most value on acquired programming like blockbuster movies, US comedy and US films. They have little interest in the more educational programmes like wildlife, science or history

7   *Review of Public Service Television Broadcasting: Phase 1*, Ofcom, 2004.

documentaries. In contrast, the over fifties consider home-grown genres very important. They rank British films and dramas very highly, whereas US programming sits at the bottom of their list. Unsurprisingly, 30–49 year olds who tend to have families value lifestyle programmes (home and DIY, food and cookery) and children's genres particularly highly.

We then analysed the genre preferences by the amount respondents are willing to pay for the BBC. The respondents who give the lowest values to the BBC (£10 and below) tend to favour entertainment and children's programmes. Respondents who are willing to pay more than £10 a month are more likely to be interested in religion, art house films and business. The respondents who attach the highest values to the BBC and who are willing to pay over £30 value programmes like children's, live action and education. These are genres which the market would not naturally provide.

So far, it is clear that the majority of the UK population value the BBC far in excess of its cost. The most enthusiastic members of the population are prepared to pay up to five times its current price and even the least enthusiastic respondents (in Scotland and Northern Ireland and those in the lower social demographics), believe on average that it is worth more than they pay for it. This does not necessarily mean, however, that the BBC should become a subscription service. When respondents are asked what they think the BBC is worth they include the value of the social benefits it provides. Unfortunately, these externalities are mostly unaccounted for when respondents are asked to think as consumers. Markets are notoriously bad at pricing citizen benefits such as the literary enthusiasm created by the *Big Read*, the understanding of ethnic minorities promoted by *Goodness Gracious Me* or the democratic debate

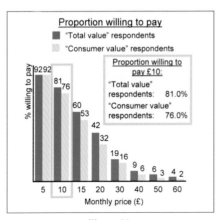

Figure 11.

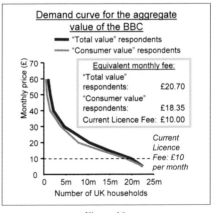

Figure 12.

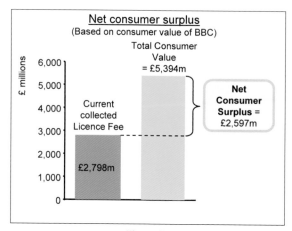

Figure 13.

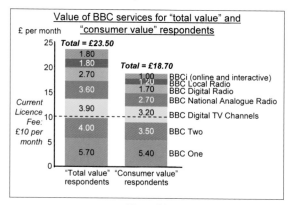

Figure 14.

encouraged by *Newsnight*.

Accordingly, respondents who were asked what they were *willing to pay* for the BBC gave lower answers than those who were asked what it is *worth* (see Figures 11 and 12). Only 76 per cent are willing to pay the current licence fee and on average they value the BBC at £18.35 per month. Admittedly, the values are not worlds apart from those given earlier and they are still much higher than £10 per month, but there *is* a significant drop. Inevitably, the net consumer surplus is slightly lower than the net citizen surplus, at £2.6bn (see Figure 13).

When respondents were asked what the BBC's services are worth to them (as opposed to society as a whole), the order of importance remains the same but each service receives a slightly lower value (see Figure 14).[8]

This research shows that the BBC is valued, on average, at twice its current cost. If it were to be sold as a subscription service, though, it would have to charge the price at which it would maximise its profit. From our research the BBC would need to charge £13 a month or £156 per year (see Figures 15, 16 and 17).

A 30 per cent price rise would not be the only consequence of subscription. Under this voluntary system only 15.2m households would participate. The 9.3m

---

8   See footnote on page 65.

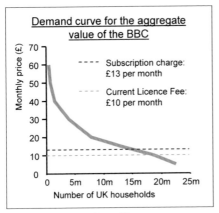

Figure 15.

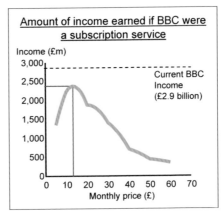

Figure 16.

Equivalent monthly fee:	
Revenue Maximising Price:	£13.00
Income:	£2.37 billion
Number of Households at £13:	15.2 million
Drop in Income at Maximising Price:	£522.7 million

Figure 17.

households who say they are not prepared to pay this much for the BBC would be quite entitled to opt-out entirely. The BBC would lose access to a third of homes or 20m people, posing a major obstacle to the scope of its public purposes.

Our research also shows that the audience members who did subscribe would tend to be English or Welsh (rather than Scottish or Northern Irish) and would be skewed to the higher demographic groups. AB respondents, for example, place the total value of the BBC at £25.65 per month, compared to the average of £20.70. This would leave the BBC in a position of preaching to the converted. The new audience would lack diversity as well as numbers.

At this point it is crucial to underline two areas which are absent from our analysis. Firstly, we have not explored the logistical difficulties which might pose as obstacles to subscription. For a start, subscription would not be possible before digital switchover. Even then, encryption would only be a definite possibility on Sky or cable operated systems. Many Freeview boxes could not be encrypted at all. Only once these were out of action could subscription actually begin. Radio would also be impossible for the foreseeable future. Online content is the only BBC service which would lend itself easily to a subscription operation.

74

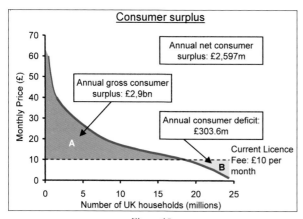

Figure 18.

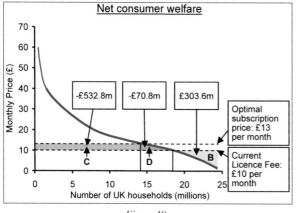

Figure 19.

Secondly, it is important to point out that we have not taken account of the respective costs of administering either the licence fee or a subscription system. Our model excludes licence fee collection and its associated costs. Subscription via encryption would most likely be a cheaper system of operation. We have not considered marketing either. Conversely, this would probably be more expensive under sub-scription. In 2004 the BBC spent £53.3m on marketing, compared to Sky's £396m.[9]

From our data it is possible to place a figure on the loss in consumer welfare which would result from subscription. Currently, with the licence fee at £10 per month there is an annual net consumer surplus of £2.6bn (see Figure 18). (That is the difference between the total amount of value which the BBC is perceived to deliver the population as consumers and the total amount of revenue collected through the licence fee.) The annual gross consumer deficit stands at £303.6m. This represents the lack of value felt by 5.9m households (shaded area B) who do not believe the BBC to be worth the cost of the licence fee. These people would benefit if the BBC went subscription because they would no longer be forced to spend their money on a service that costs more than they think it is worth.

Figure 19 above shows how the majority of the population would lose out. Those

---

9   *BBC Annual Report*, 2004 and *Sky Annual Report*, 2004.

Area on the graph (Figure 19)	Monthly value placed on BBC	Size of group (households)	How would they be affected by a £13 voluntary monthly subscription charge?	Welfare gain/loss
B	< £10	5.9m	They consider the BBC poor value for money so they are currently unhappy paying £10. At £13 they would be better off as they could choose not to subscribe.	£303.6m
D	£10-13	3.8m	They are currently happy paying £10. At £13 they would choose not to subscribe and lose out on what was a good value service.	-£70.8m
C	£13 +	14.8m	They currently get excellent value from the BBC. It costs them £10 a month but they think it is worth much more. They would end up paying more money and would lose out by £3 per household.	-£532.8m

Figure 20.

who value the BBC at £10 but not £13 (shaded area D) would opt-out of subscribing, losing a service they had once valued. Their total loss of welfare would be £70.8m. The final group (shaded area C) who value the BBC at £13 or over would end up paying more money for the same service. Their loss would be £532.8m. The total welfare loss would be around £300m a year or £25m a month.

Even at the increased charge of £13, the smaller number of participating households would lower the annual revenue of the BBC by £522.7m to £2.37bn. With these reduced funds it is likely that the quality of output would be compromised. In order to increase its income and broaden its audience, the BBC, like any other commercial broadcaster, would more than likely seek to focus on the genres which would drive subscription, namely movies and sports. As a result, the BBC would end up being a very different broadcaster.

If subscription is intended to stop people being forced to pay for something they do not want, then it goes without saying that different subscription packages ought to be made available in order to cater for the tastes and needs of different households. We have calculated the cost of various combinations of services at the prices where they would maximise revenue.[10]

Figure 21 below shows how much the BBC would charge for its channels as subscription packages. If these were the only packages on offer 58 per cent of households (14m) would opt out entirely.

---

10 Radio has been ignored on the basis that there is no easy way to sell it on a subscription basis.

Service package	Monthly subscription price	Percentage of consumers who would subscribe	Number of households	Annual revenue
BBC One	£7	4%	0.9m	£75m
BBC One + BBC Two	£9	17%	4.1m	£438m
BBC One + BBC Two + BBC digital channels	£11	22%	5.5m	£719m
Opt out of all packages	N/A	58%	14m	N/A
TOTAL	N/A	100%	24.5m	£1,232m

Figure 21.

Our research shows that the population is overwhelmingly in favour of the BBC at its current price. On average, it is valued at twice its cost (£240 a year) and every one of its constituent services is considered to deliver more value than it costs. This is particularly true of the digital channels which generate remarkable value for money by operating from an exceptionally low cost base. High-quality programming is considered to be essential in driving value and of the BBC's programmes, news, regional news and soaps are seen as the most important. As a subscription service the BBC would set a revenue-maximising price of £13 per month (a 30 per cent increase). As a consequence, we estimate it would lose touch with 9.3m of the 24.5m homes. This lack of universality would undermine the BBC's ability to carry out its public purposes. Overall, subscription would bring in £500m a year less than the licence fee, causing a potential downturn in quality. Over and above this, the population as a whole would lose £300m of consumer welfare every year.

References

Spectrum Strategy Consultants and Indepen for the British Library, *Measuring our Value*, 2003.

T.B. Hansen, 'The willingness-to-pay for the Royal Theatre in Copenhagen as a public good', in *Journal of Cultural Economics*, 21, 1–28, 1997.

Home Office Study (1987), *Subscription Television: A Study for the Home Office* A. Ehrenberg and P. Mills, *Viewers' Willingness to Pay* (London Business School), 1990.

Radio-communications Agency/DTI, *Survey to determine the consumers' surplus accruing to TV viewers and radio listeners*, 2000.

Research on broadcaster value abroad: CBC, Canada (2000) and RTE, Ireland (2003).

The Future of Funding the BBC – Report of the Independent Review Panel, (DCMS) 1999.

Ofcom, *Review of Public Service Television Broadcasting, Phase 1 – Is Television Special?*, 2004.

Ofcom, *Review of Public Service Television Broadcasting, Phase 2 – Meeting the Digital Challenge*, 2004.

5

'It's the Ecology, Stupid'

Andrew Graham[1]

Introduction: from Peacock to Ofcom

Two interlinked discussions are currently underway: the study of public service broadcasting (PSB) by Ofcom and debate about the renewal of the BBC's Charter due in 2006. To make sense of the flood of new material, it helps to look back nearly twenty years to the Charter renewal of 1986 and especially to the Peacock Report that accompanied it. That report marked the first serious questioning of the existence of the BBC and placed in front of everyone the view that, as the digital revolution occurred, broadcasting should become primarily determined by market forces.

Of course the debate has moved on since Peacock. In particular there have been substantive critiques of Peacock, the BBC successfully achieved a further Charter renewal in 1996 and, following the report of the Davies Panel of 1999, was granted a boost in its funding. Nonetheless, the same two strands of argument have defined the agenda right up to the present. In essence, there are those who argue that broadcasting should move to being predominantly a commercial activity versus those who maintain that broadcasting displays special characteristics and that a substantial role for PSB is still required.

This essay examines the current debate primarily through the lens of these two opposing views. First, the views of Peacock and the early critiques of that

---

1 The views expressed here are personal and have no necessary link with those of Channel 4. I would also like to thank Peggotty Graham for perceptive comments on an earlier version.

What about the scale of the BBC? On this point, too, those who regard the BBC as too large are unconvincing. To see why, it is necessary to distinguish (i) scale relative to what from (ii) the grounds on which scale might be a concern.

On the question of *scale relative to what*, Figure 1 (facing) is instructive. The top line shows the BBC and for the last twenty years, relative to the broadcasting market as a whole, the BBC has been getting smaller, not larger. It is only relative to ITV that the BBC has become larger (with the BBC in 2003 and 2004 at some 38 per cent compared to ITV at about 24 per cent). However, this is entirely because of the decline in ITV, falling from being equivalent to the BBC in the early 1980s, to less than two-thirds now.

The arguments about scale are equally unconvincing when we consider the *reasons* why the critics of the BBC are concerned about its size. Broadcasting, we are told, suffers from 'two powerful monopolies, the BBC ... and Sky'.[12] However, for a monopoly to be undesirable, prices must be high or there must be restrictions on choice or there must be abuses of power.

In the case of prices, the licence fee is only £10 per month (compared to some £30 per month for a typical Sky package). In the case of choice, one of the BBC's purposes is to make programmes that are different (either in their subject matter or their treatment) from those of the commercial broadcasters. The BBC therefore *adds* to choice.

Does the BBC abuse its power? There are two possibilities here. First, there is the power of the BBC as a purchaser: not its monopoly power but its monopsony power. This part of the argument does have merit. There is evidence that the independent producers, especially the smaller ones, have had to accept terms less attractive than those they would have received in a more competitive market. However, these issues have already been addressed, at least in part, following a review by the ITC.[13]

Second is the more serious accusation that the BBC damages 'democratic pluralism',[14] that it acts as a 'cultural tyranny' and as 'propagating a unifying cultural force'.[15] But where is the evidence? None is produced and indeed Cox himself agrees that the BBC is 'largely benevolent'.[16] In any case, the BBC is

---

12 Cox, B. (2004) p. 16.

13 Independent Television Commission (ITC) *Programme Supply Review*, 2002.

14 Elstein, D. (2004) p. 5.

15 Cox, B. (2004) pp. 61, 69 respectively.

16 Cox, B. (2004) p. 61. In fact Cox's real concern seems to be not with the BBC's tyranny of programmes, but with the fact that the Board of Governors is not democratically accountable – an entirely different point.

explicitly required to be impartial. As a result, on almost all of the major issues facing society, the BBC is one of the main places in which a *diversity* of views can be found, including voices from many different parts of the UK's contemporary cultural mix. Indeed, it was the BBC who prepared a report on the current UK as divided into a 'hundred tribes' as Cox himself reports. Not much propagation of cultural unity there.

There is one further major echo of what we might call the 'market optimism' of the Peacock report which needs to be assessed. This is the claim that, in the digital age, the primary instrument of broadcasting policy should be regulation that promotes competition. The Communications White Paper of 2003 stated that Ofcom was to be charged with 'protecting the interest of consumers in terms of choice, price, quality of service and value for money, in particular through promoting open and competitive markets' and Ofcom has subsequently argued that 'a structural tendency towards monopoly ... is an issue best addressed by competition policy'.[17]

There are four grounds for doubting the effectiveness of regulation in broadcasting. First, new technology generates powerful economies of scale (because, in the digital age, the second copy costs nothing) and economies of scope (because of convergence). To exploit the first, there will be large firms. To exploit the second, there will be many channels (and other outlets), *but only few owners*. Added to these are the economics of networks and standards which will also push towards concentration. In other words, regulation may be trying to be pro-competitive, but it will be walking up an escalator that is going down.

Second, regulators attempting to tackle positions of power risk long and expensive lawsuits. This can be especially so where regulators act *ex ante* since the claim that market dominance *will* exist and *will* be abused may prove more difficult to sustain than one that points to the existence of actual dominance or abuse.

Third, there are times when, in the interests of promoting technical change or the promulgation of standards, regulators are only too willing to see dominance come into existence (as has happened with Microsoft and Sky).

The fact that dominance is allowed or even encouraged leads to the fourth reason for relying too heavily on regulation to promote competition – it can take an inordinately long time to achieve this. For example, it took more than ten years

---

17 Ofcom (2004a) *Ofcom review of public service broadcasting, Phase 1 – Is television special?* Ofcom, para. 153.

for the telephone monopoly in the USA to be broken up – and this was ten years after the case for breaking it up had been established.

In this context it is worth observing, albeit somewhat ironically, two features of the current debate. One is that Cox is full of how much, alongside the BBC, Sky is part of the double monopoly (and, by implication, of how much that should be tackled). The other is that, when we turn to the various reports by Ofcom, Sky merits hardly a mention. It would, of course, be wrong to subscribe unthinkingly to some of the more rabid conspiracy theories about the role of Mr. Murdoch, but it would be equally unthinking not to take account of what the primary sources show us. For example, Woodrow Wyatt's journals report Irwin Stelzer, a consultant to News Corp, as saying '[Murdoch]'s got Blair not to mention the possible reference of the BSkyB to the Monopolies Commission'.[18] To put the same point another way, why do 'market optimists' believe the new regulators will be so effective in their pro-competitive vigilance, when the evidence from the past suggests a far more complex picture?

The reason this matters is not merely because of the *negative* point that regulation may be ineffective. There is also the *positive* point that one important role for public service broadcasters is to act as counterweights to monopoly power elsewhere. Indeed it is Ofcom who have observed that in the past 'The BBC kept ITV honest; ITV kept the BBC on its toes. Channel 4 energised the mix, bringing in a whole new group of independent producers'.[19] This is not only an excellent summary of why the ecology of UK broadcasting has been so successful, but also displays how inappropriate is the assumption that the BBC monopoly is just as undesirable as the Sky monopoly. The 'market optimists' may wish that the world could be a different place so that not only were there many channels but also many owners, but that is not the world we face. There is a good case for encouraging, but it is bad policy to throw away something that has worked (the positive influence of the BBC on the broadcasting market) in favour of the purely imagined benefits of a policy (pro-competitive regulation) that has not yet been shown to work effectively. When you have a belt and braces, neither perfectly reliable, why only use one of them?

The empirical evidence on consumer value

The points above suggest that many of the arguments made in response to Peacock in favour of public service broadcasting continue to be valid. There is,

---

18 Woodrow, W. (1999) 'Journal for 1 December 1995', *The Journals of Woodrow Wyatt: Volume One.* Pan.

19 Ofcom (2004a) p. 2.

however, one major question that has, so far, not been considered. Are the resources devoted to PSB – and these include not just the BBC, but also the subsidies to free spectrum and the obligations on C4 and ITV – too large for the simple reason that PSB is valued by much less than the cost of PSB which Ofcom put at some £3 billion?

The question of the value of PSB has to be answered at a number of levels. The first and most obvious one is 'how much do *consumers* value the BBC?' The more problematic ones concern how to assess the value of all of PSB to society. We shall return to these below.

The first major study of the value consumers place on the BBC was that by Ehrenberg and Mills (1990). They found that 90 per cent of people would have been willing to pay a subscription just above the then licence fee to receive BBC One and BBC Two. Allowing for a positive value to BBC radio and for the fact that, within the 90 per cent, there would have been many willing to pay more, this suggested that the BBC was valued substantially more than the revenue needed to operate it.

Recent work reinforces this conclusion. Research carried out by the BBC and Human Capital (see Chapter 4) have found that, while the current licence fee is £10 per month, consumers valued the BBC at approximately £18 per month.[20] Human Capital have also made estimates of the overall shape of the demand curve for the services of the BBC. This allows them to carry out the correct kind of analysis for a public good, which is to add up the whole area under the demand curve. The overall result is a consumer value of £5.4 billion – or nearly twice the current revenue from the licence fee and substantially above Ofcom's estimate of the total cost of PSB of £3 billion.

Market failures beyond public goods

So far we have considered the value of the BBC in terms of the value that consumers would place on it when it is measured as a 'public good'. This is a useful move, but it is not sufficient to measure the value, either of the BBC or of the whole of PSB, to society.

One reason why the consumer valuation is not sufficient is that there are effects that consumers will not include in their valuations. These 'externalities' can be either negative (e.g. from smokers) or positive (e.g. from vaccinations). Where

20 BBC/Human Capital (2004) *Measuring the value of the BBC – A report by the BBC and Human Capital.* BBC.

externalities are negative the consumer value will overstate the value to society, where positive it will understate it.

Does broadcasting exhibit externalities and, if so, are these positive or negative? In a major study, Hamilton (1998) has shown that broadcasting externalities can be either large and negative (e.g. from the depiction of violence) or large and positive (e.g. from educational programmes). Other examples of programmes with negative externalities would be those that demeaned particular groups in society, whereas programmes that projected authentic representations or those that encouraged mutual understanding between different cultures or those that contributed to 'social capital' would have positive externalities.[21] Since one of the main purposes of PSB is to produce programmes that have positive externalities, the value of PSB to society will be *above* what consumers will estimate.

A second reason why the consumer valuation is not sufficient is because of 'merit goods'. These are goods that consumers will realize, but only later in their lives, that they value much more than they currently think.[22] Education is an example. So are programmes which may not look 'educational' but which are mind or experience-expanding. By the same token, programmes that are literally mind-numbingly repetitive would be 'de-merit' goods.

Critics of this viewpoint suggest either that we cannot identify merit (or de-merit) goods or that, if they exist, the decision to embody them in programmes and to broadcast them in ways in which people are encouraged to watch (e.g. by 'hammocking' them between other highly popular programmes) represents undesirable paternalism. Neither argument convinces. The first presupposes that we are completely incapable of making judgements about the quality of programmes or that some programmes will not stand the test of time better than others. The second denies that we learn from experience and come to value things differently because of the experience. Yet it is well established that, following education, many people earn more than they initially expected. The corollary is that, if they had known this, they would have been willing to pay more for it than they initially thought.

Putting the point more generally, in many aspects of life we recognize that 'the company we keep' can have powerful effects on our potential. That is why, if

---

21 Brookes, M. (2004) discusses the many ways in which PSB can add to social capital.

22 Sometimes 'later' can be as short as the distance before and after the programme. Once seen, people realize they value the programme more than they initially expected. Sometimes 'later' may be many years – programmes such as *Live Aid* or *Cathy Come Home* continue to reverberate.

given a choice, we would all want people to be in a good school or a good team or a good firm. It may sound tautological that we would choose the 'good', but if the quality of these institutions made no difference, we would not judge them as good or bad. The fact that we all evaluate schools, teams, universities and firms in this way is precisely because, *after we have been in them*, we are acutely aware of the consequences of better or worse environments.[23] The relevance of this to broadcasting is that television is watched, on average, about twenty five hours per week. Broadcasting is, therefore, a substantial part the 'company we keep'.

To return to the issue of valuing PSB, we should expect PSBs to broadcast more programmes having the characteristics of merit goods than commercial broadcasters. Given this and given that consumers undervalue merit goods, their existence is a further reason why the value of PSB to society will be *above* what consumers, thinking just about themselves, will estimate. Interestingly, research by Ofcom suggests that viewers are aware of this. When asked, not what they would choose, but 'What is the best TV for society?' the majority of the group chose the option characterized by 'It's good for all of us to be surprised and stretched'.[24]

The role of the citizen – the theory of political rights

The case so far made for PSB has been based primarily on the existence of 'public goods', 'externalities' and 'merit goods'. These are all market failures. The case for PSB is not, however, restricted to these.[25] The second fundamental justification for PSBs derives from democratic theory and especially from the theory of political rights.

At the core of democratic theory is the belief, subscribed to by all democratic societies, that resources may justifiably be allocated according to two different principles. In the marketplace one person's pound is as good as another's, whereas in the public arena one person's vote is as good as another's. Moreover, it is generally acknowledged in liberal societies that citizenship entails a range of rights beyond the mere casting of votes. These include the right to information

---

23 We may have some awareness of this beforehand, but, rarely, to the full extent.

24 Ofcom (2004c) p. 17.

25 Regrettably, in my view, the Davies Report (1999) helped give credence to the view that 'market failure' was the only justification for PSB. With economic analysis so dominant at the time, this may have been an astute short run move, but, analytically, it is a mistake and none of our earlier joint work would support this view.

about how the society is governed and about the law, the right to participate fully in that society and the right to equality of respect.[26]

The realization of these rights is increasingly dependent upon the media. For the right to information about society to have meaning it should be free, not sold for profit via the television or the PC. The right to participate increasingly requires that views are promulgated as much on television as on the floor of the House of Commons; and, as for respect, broadcasting has become the dominant way in which different parts of society present themselves (or are presented) to each other.

Ofcom's analysis of PSB hardly mentions rights.[27] In their Phase 1 report on PSB the thrust of the analysis is almost entirely on market failure.[28] It is true that citizens feature but they do so largely as what might be described as 'consumers with the market corrected'. For example, it is said that 'The citizen-focused objectives can be seen as those measures needed to make sure television delivers sufficient positive externalities and merit goods' and then it continues, somewhat puzzlingly since the distribution of income has not featured before, that this will be done 'by giving *all* citizens access to programming of wider social value (emphasis added)'.[29] Perhaps this is rights by the back door, but, if so, it is very low key. Moreover, the only mention of those with 'low purchasing' is in a footnote[30] where is it conceded that they might be under-served by advertisers.[31]

Despite this lack of attention to rights, there is recent empirical work that casts some light on the issue. Human Capital, as mentioned above, has made estimates of the 'consumer value' of the BBC. In addition, they have attempted to measure what they call its 'total value'. Prompted by the observation that resources can be allocated by pounds or votes, Human Capital constructed a study in which respondents were asked to vote for continuing the licence fee at various levels. In another part of the study they asked a similar question but

26   The International Covenants on Economic, Social and Cultural Rights and on Civil and Political Rights adopted by the General Assembly of the UN in 1966 specify the rights of every citizen to the protection of the law, to participate in the conduct of public affairs and to respect for privacy.

27   Ofcom (2004a) para. 95. The only reference I could find was where viewers brought it up, regarding their access to the terrestrial channels to be a 'right'.

28   See especially Ofcom (2004a) paras 137–170.

29   Ofcom (2004a) para. 147.

30   Ofcom (2004a) Footnote 32.

31   Ofcom (2004a) It is hard to know what to make of para. 148 which says that the broad social purposes of PSB 'should be widely available to all citizens' when this is followed by para. 156 which says 'If [reaching large numbers of people] is no longer possible in a digital world … the case for continued PSB would be much diminished'.

channel by channel. In Human Capital's view those replying were in no doubt that they were being asked to think about the *overall* value of the BBC to society at large. In these circumstances, even though respondents may never have heard of 'externalities' or 'merit goods' nor thought much about rights, their replies might include an allowance for these factors – at least to some degree. If so, and if we take the BBC as representing PSB, then we should expect to find larger values than those for pure 'consumer value'. This is exactly what occurs. The total value figures for the BBC as a whole were just over £20 per month on the national voting approach and those derived channel by channel were £23.50 – both significantly above the consumer value mentioned earlier of £18. Moreover, the area under the curve also goes up – to just over £6 billion.

A second piece of evidence comes from the research conducted by Ofcom itself. In this case respondents took part in discussion and recorded their views at various stages. The purpose of the research was to find out how much value, *both monetary and evaluative*, viewers placed upon PSB. Inevitably with deliberative research, the findings were rich, complex and not easily quantifiable. Nevertheless, amongst the points that stood out in the views of participants were:

(i)   The licence fee was seen as the best compromise choice for funding PSB;

(ii)   They felt that the overall level of funding for PSB should rise from its present annual level of £121 to somewhere between £121 and £151;

(iii)   They had a clear sense that television could be good for society and 'some form of intervention would continue to be necessary' to bring this about;[32]

(iv)   While Ofcom may not have spoken or thought in terms of 'rights', the participants used language, apparently without prompting, which springs from such thinking. While recognizing that viewers could be 'passive' or 'supine' they also felt that television had a role in society that was 'vital in the discursive process of democracy'.[33]

Whilst considering political rights, one further point should be noted. The two theories from which the case for PSBs is derived – market failure and democratic rights – stand independent of one another. However, they are also strongly complementary. This can clearly be seen if we realise the extent to which PSB, far from hindering the market or restricting choice, helps both. It is often

---

32   Ofcom (2004c) p. 54.
33   Ofcom (2004c) p. 54.

forgotten that the theory of consumer choice, on which the claim in favour of a free market in broadcasting rests, presupposes consumers who are already both fully *formed* (they know their own preferences), and fully *informed*. In reality, neither is likely. As a result, and given that the media is one of the main sources of information as well as one of the ways in which people come to understand themselves, the existence of a set of broadcasters committed to empowering citizens and providing impartial information is a prerequisite for market efficiency.

The argument so far and moving beyond the revealed demand curve

Up to this point, we have done three things. First, we have noted that the estimate of pure *consumer* value suggested that viewers would be willing to pay a licence fee of about £18 per month. This was measuring the BBC just as a public good. Second, we have seen that three further factors need to be taken into account: externalities, merit goods and political rights. Third, a possible measure of *total* demand, which would go some way to include externalities, merit goods and political rights, suggested that people would pay a licence fee of, perhaps, £23.50 per month and that the total value would be some £6 billion, or twice the current cost of PSB at £3 billion.

There are, however, three powerful reasons why even the total demand figure estimated so far is likely to give too low a figure for the value of PSB to society.

First, as explained, merit goods are valued at a higher level than first expected in the light of a full appreciation of their beneficial outcomes. However, those responding to the research will be representative samples (or as near to that as can be achieved). If so, some of them will have had little exposure to merit goods. Such people will, of necessity, undervalue merit goods. It follows that representative samples are bound to undervalue PSB.

Second, a similar argument applies to programmes that exhibit positive externalities. These are, again, the kinds of programmes that PSBs should be making. However, it is in the very nature of an externality that some of the benefits accrue elsewhere, so the individual does not value it sufficiently.

Third, the role of PSBs in delivering rights and in helping to encourage democracy is also likely to be underestimated. As Hirschman (1982) has pointed out, we regularly place too low a value on things *because they are taken for granted*. He gave as one example, glass in windows. It is just there and we cannot remember what winters must have been like without it. The same may well be true of democracy. Few people living in Western Europe aged less than sixty will have any memories of fascist or totalitarian regimes, and in the UK and the USA, apart from recent immigrants, only a tiny minority has any relevant memory at all. In contrast, we know that people who lack democracy value it so highly that some of them will lay down their lives for it.

It might be replied that the research conducted by both Human Capital and by Ofcom has captured these effects. This would seem to be especially true of Human Capital's attempt to measure *total* value. Ofcom's question about what is the best TV for society also heads in this direction. Indeed it can be readily agreed that both of these are moves in the direction that theory would suggest. What cannot be agreed is that these moves are sufficient.

The reason these moves cannot be sufficient is because of the highly demanding nature of the assumptions. For the individuals replying either to Ofcom or to Human Capital to have captured *fully* the value to society of PSB, *it would be necessary for them to be both perfectly informed and perfectly altruistic*. The assumption about information is required for them (a) to understand fully *all* the external effects and (b) to forecast the merit good effects. The assumption about altruism is required in order that, having understood and forecast accurately, they would then be able to place themselves completely in the position of 'the other'.

It should be immediately clear that these assumptions are not merely demanding, but manifestly not attainable. Perfect information is a figment of some economic theories, but no more than that and perfect altruism is something that would strain the imagination of almost anyone, let alone economists. If this is not sufficient to make the point, readers familiar with the history of social science will know that some of its most profound thinkers, such as Adam Smith or John Rawls, have advocated thought experiments of these kinds – especially that of putting oneself in the position of others. However, what no-one has ever argued is that representative respondents to a survey would do this, still less that they would do it spontaneously. They might reach towards it, as some of the respondents to Ofcom appeared to do, but they can hardly be expected to achieve it fully.

Figure 2 (below) summarises the points above. We start with a consumer value (the area under Curve 1) of some £5 billion. By definition, public service programmes are those which, on balance, contain more merit goods and more positive externalities than those produced by the market. These two effects must therefore increase the value to society of PSB programmes. To this we add the theory of political rights – a further need for PSB. One estimate of this is the 'total value' of the BBC of, perhaps £6 billion (the area under Curve2). Finally,

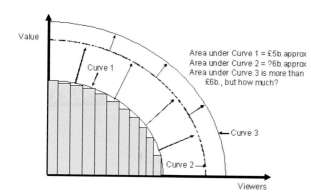

Figure 2. Curve 1 is consumer value. Curve 2 is above Curve 1 with partial allowance for externalities, merit goods and rights. Curve 3 with full allowance will be higher, but how much higher?

it has been argued that respondents to surveys will underestimate on all three counts. In aggregate, therefore, the demand for PSB across society as a whole must be even larger – this is represented by Curve 3 – but we do not know exactly how much.

How is PSB to be achieved? Ofcom's answer

Faced with the fact that there is both substantial support amongst the public for the *idea* of public service broadcasting and that viewers appear to value PSB significantly above the revenue currently raised by the licence fee, Ofcom have faced a quandary. They could hardly advocate giving extra PSB money to ITV as they had already argued that the new competitive pressures in broadcasting were causing ITV to shed its PSB obligations.

Another solution would be more funding for the BBC. However, based on work by Schlesinger, which argued in favour of a plurality of institutions, Ofcom concluded that this, too, would be unacceptable.[34] One cannot tell how much Ofcom may also have been influenced by the prevalent view that the BBC is already too large, though it is not difficult to imagine that this, too, will have played a role.

The second home for more PSB funding might have been Channel 4. This might have had a number of attractions to Ofcom. Channel 4 already has public service obligations in its remit, it is much smaller than the BBC (so building it up would have increased competition between the PSBs) and it was favourably perceived in the research conducted by Ofcom. Nevertheless, any inclination that Ofcom

34 Schlesinger, P. (2004) *Do Institutions Matter for Public Service Broadcasting?* Research paper prepared for Ofcom.

might have shown to go in this direction appears to have stumbled on *how* this might be done.

Another alternative which they considered was the Peacock/Cox/Elstein proposal for a Public Broadcasting Authority (PBA) distributing funds between competing propositions. However, Ofcom rejected this because it would be costly (with commissioning editors being duplicated by the PBA and those bidding) and because they were worried whether PSB programmes funded in this way would achieve adequate distribution and whether the programmes would be found by viewers.

Faced with no clear 'home' for the extra funding, and with the PBA being rejected, Ofcom's proposal is that a sum of money, which they put at 'up to £300 million' by 2012, should be set aside to establish a new animal. They call this a Public Service Publisher (PSP). It would, they suggest, 'aim to commission and distribute content as widely as possible'.[35] It would not, they say, be a TV channel in the traditional sense, but existing broadcasters (except for the BBC) would be able to bid to run it. So also would other organizations, but anyone receiving such funds would have to ring fence them from other commercial operations. Alternatively, the PSP might be a new stand-alone provider.

There are several reasons why the suggestion of creating a new PSP probably seemed attractive to Ofcom. One is that it would appear to increase the amount of competition amongst PSBs. Ofcom could therefore have ticked this box. Another box that Ofcom would have been able to tick is that of transparency. By making the funding for this clearly identifiable and separate from any existing institution, they would have achieved the open and direct subsidy that economists have been hankering for ever since Peacock. In addition, they probably wanted to give the money to a body which had a clearly defined objective, rather than, as they see it, to the too broad-reaching and confused objectives that exist within the BBC or Channel 4.

Despite these attractions, there are, however, some substantial unresolved questions and potential difficulties with the Ofcom solution of a PSP. The first is the lack of clarity in the proposal. Since the idea remains at the level of consultation, perhaps this was intentional. Nevertheless, it is difficult to see how it can be both a commissioner and a distributor and yet not be a channel. On the other hand, if it is not a channel or is not part of an existing channel, there must be questions about how it will establish itself as a brand.

---

35 Ofcom (2004b) para. 6.35.

This question of the brand leads directly to the second difficulty. Would a stand-alone PSP be large enough on the scale proposed to be recognizable by the audience? On today's numbers Channel 4 is already more than twice as large and the BBC is nearly ten times the size. By 2012 even a budget that looks as substantial as 'up to £300 million' will be relatively small compared to the two incumbent PSBs with whom the PSP would need to compete.[36] Thus any tick in that box that Ofcom may have given must have a question mark against it. In any case, a PSP on this scale sits rather oddly with Ofcom's earlier agreement that Carlton and Granada should merge because they needed to be larger in order to compete.

A third problem with the PSP, especially in its stand-alone form, is the danger that the existence of this specialist public service entity would take the pressure off the other broadcasters to produce public service programmes, thus undermining rather than strengthening PSB overall. Moreover, this weakness is linked to two others. One is that the presence of a PSP might ghetto-ise PSB. This would be a disaster and would run counter to everything that the ecology of British broadcasting has so far achieved. The other is that, if the PSP came to be seen as a specialist activity, its audience sizes would collapse. In short, there must be a danger that the existence of a stand-alone PSP would push PSB in the UK into the same tiny irrelevant niche that it occupies in the USA.

The role of public institutions and joint objectives

To see more clearly *why* a stand-alone PSP would be a mistake, it is necessary to understand something about the character of good public service broadcasting that is rarely made explicit. Good PSB consists of programmes that both *stretch* people and *reach* people. Moreover, this is much more than the fact that, having made a programme, it is nice to have viewers. It is that the desire to reach people influences the stretching and vice versa. An analogy with universities makes the point. The goal of a university is both to create knowledge and to disseminate it and the two feed on each other. Of course, as many in universities and in broadcasting are well aware, managing joint objectives, neither of which is easily measured or reduced to a line in the P&L account, is problematic. Sometimes the complementarity is clear, easy and highly productive (e.g. when the need to explain an idea exposes a flaw in accepted

36 There might well be a useful role for a PSP acting as an innovator, especially perhaps experimenting with new media. However, (a) such work would, at most, be only part of the £300 million and (b) in this part of its role the PSP could not possibly compete with the BBC and Channel 4 *as channels*.

theory or when the need to connect with an audience means that the stretching works), while at other times the competition for resources of time, energy and money is intense. Nevertheless the success, the manifest quality and the global appeal of British broadcasting suggest that, on balance, the two objectives have fed on one another successfully.

What is being suggested by this argument is that Ofcom may not have fully understood the peculiar genius of Reithian broadcasting. Far from Reith's injunction to the BBC that it should 'inform, educate and entertain' displaying a dangerous confusion of purpose which must now be unpacked in the interests of 'transparency' and of solving what economists call the 'principal/agent' problem, it was tying together activities that, much of the time, benefited one another. Indeed, it is worth recalling that when ITV was first created in 1955 under the then ITA, it was given the very same injunction; and when Channel 4 was formed in 1982, its particular status – charged with PSB obligations, but wholly dependent on advertising revenue – embodied precisely the tension between stretch and reach.

Moreover, the need to straddle, however uncomfortably, these two positions will increase, not decrease as the digital revolution proceeds. In the past, programmes that might stretch viewers could be 'hammocked' between two programmes with popular appeal. However, as channels proliferate and as the technology makes it ever easier for viewers to design their own watching, the stretching and reaching will need, even more than now, to be *within* programmes (an example where this worked well was the *Great Britons* programme).

While, therefore, Ofcom has been right to reject the Broadcasting Council model and to emphasise the need for long term funding, they are probably wrong to suggest that the PSP might be successful as a stand-alone model. Unless the public service obligations exist within an institution that is also committed to reaching people, sometimes using all the techniques of the commercial broadcasters, there seems little hope that this part of the UK's successful ecology will survive.

At the same time it must be recognized that it is difficult to keep complex institutions on track and Barry Cox has rightly emphasized the strains on the ethos of the BBC with some feeling themselves 'second-class citizens' if they are not making hugely popular programmes. But, while the strains have increased, they are not new and whether people feel like this is substantially a matter of leadership and management. The extent and speed of the re-vivification of the

BBC that occurred when Greg Dyke became Director General shows what can be done.[37]

Handling the strains of competing objectives also requires good governance. In the wake of Hutton and in the current anti-BBC mood, the instinctive reaction of most people is to say that the Board of Governors should either be abolished or their obligations should be substantially reduced and, instead, the BBC should be brought within the purview of the all-purpose communications regulator, Ofcom. There is some force in this in the sense that it is extremely difficult, some would say impossible, for the BBC Governors to be, at one and the same time, acting like the board of a company and acting like a regulator.

As always, however, glib conclusions need to be resisted. Four considerations, in particular, point in a different direction. First, in the Communications Act 2003 many of the formal regulatory mechanisms, such as the policing of competition, are already the responsibility of Ofcom and not that of the Governors. This is as it should be and no *further* transfer of powers is required to achieve this.

Second, consider the Gilligan Affair: no *external* regulator would have been able to prevent this. Or, if they had, they would have been engaging in a degree of micro-management that would look almost Stalinist. So, it is only *internal* editorial controls plus the ex-post investigation that is at issue. The first can and should be done by the BBC's management and there is no reason why the Board of Governors could not do the second. Indeed, from now on, the danger is that the Governors will over-regulate and over-inquire. Once bitten will be much more than twice shy.

Third, recall the fundamental reason for having PSBs: it is for programmes to be made that have different criteria from those of the market – to present an authentic picture, to promote our understanding, to stimulate us, to make us laugh without demeaning others and so on. But regulators do not make programmes. Regulators can only *stop* things; they cannot *produce* things. The crucial people are the commissioning editors and the producers, and these people have to exist within an institution that encourages them and maintains the ethos of PSB.[38] This is what the Board of Governors should do and, if they have not, they have been failing, but this is not a failure than can possibly be corrected by taking the responsibility for PSB away from the Governors. Such an argument is wholly fallacious. Anyone putting it forward has not understood

---

37 See Born, G. (2004) *Uncertain Vision: Birt, Dyke and the Reinvention of the BBC*. London: Secker and Warburg.

38 As Graham and Davies (1992) argued and as Schlesinger (2004) has confirmed.

why PSBs are needed. Writing as a non-executive director of Channel 4, with direct observation on the one hand of the Independent Television Commission (ITC) (the former regulator of Channel 4) and on the other hand of the commissioning editors of Channel 4, it is totally clear that Channel 4 would not work if the ITC had been the direct regulator of Channel 4's editors. This has to be a matter for the Board.

Fourth, there is a danger to a democracy in placing too much power in the hands of a single regulator. Regulators can be monopolists just as much as firms, and a monopoly of *values* is far more threatening to a society than the monopoly of a single product. In the UK, Ofcom already combines no fewer than five former regulators (the Broadcasting Standards Commission, the ITC, Oftel, the Radio Authority and the Radiocommunications Agency). To add any more would be a step too far.

The way forward

In thinking about the way forward, it is useful to start by giving credit to the substantial research that has been carried out and particularly to Ofcom's discussion of PSB. Its two reports, especially Phase 2, have moved the debate forward substantially. What this work shows is that the case *in principle* for PSB has been made and that it is valued *in practice*. Moreover, it has proved to be valued at a higher level than many (including Ofcom?) may have first thought.

The next point is that there is no reason for the BBC to decline. This is fundamental because exactly the opposite assumption has been made by Cox and Elstein as well as, it would seem, by Ofcom in Phase 1 and its research leading to Phase 2. The crucial point is this: most industry projections do, indeed, show the BBC as declining, but they do so only by using a wholly unjustified assumption. They assume that 'other broadcasting revenue' (i.e from advertising, subscription, sponsorship and pay-per-view) is projected to grow faster than the licence fee. Why? Because the licence fee is assumed constant in real terms, whereas the other parts of broadcasting display positive income elasticity. But, *what the licence fee does is a policy decision*. If it were decided that the licence fee would grow as fast as other revenues, the BBC would not decline. No amount of sophistry should hide this.

What about plurality of view? This is a powerful point and competition *within* the public sector is just as healthy as it is in the private sector. The only problem, and it is a real problem, lies in economies of scale. You may (just) be able to have more than one hundred universities, but you cannot have even ten PSBs, and probably not more than two or three – at least not viable ones.

What ought to be done is threefold.

First, there should be no rush to remove the PSB obligations on the ITV companies. On the contrary, any moves that slowed down the shedding of their obligations should be welcomed.

Second, we should welcome a strong BBC and appreciate the significant role it still has to play as a 'standard setter'. Moreover, if this role is to be preserved, its revenues need to grow, not diminish.

Third, the merits of Channel 4 mentioned in Ofcom's research should be recognised. Channel 4 already receives implicit public support via its access to free spectrum. That should continue and be guaranteed to continue beyond switchover. And, if further support is needed, as Ofcom appears to think, it seems difficult to suppose that a way could not be found in which this could be done without infringing the channel's widely- recognised commitments to innovation and diversity. On some readings, Ofcom's proposal for a PSP is almost saying this.

Beyond this, there is probably a good case for a reform of the governance of the BBC in the limited sense of reconsidering what *sort* of Governors are needed. They are not meant to be representatives of the great and the good nor of the UK's geography. They are meant to be capable of taking a strategic view of the BBC, as non-executive directors do for any company, to be people who have shown that they understand what public service broadcasting is about and to have the willingness to uphold that ethos within the BBC.

None of this is radical. That is its strength, not its weakness. Like other ecologies, the UK's broadcasting ecology will be best preserved by evolution not revolution.

References

BBC/Human Capital (2004) *Measuring the Value of the BBC – A report by the BBC and Human Capital.* BBC.

Born, G. (2004) *Uncertain Vision: Birt, Dyke and the Reinvention of the BBC.* London: Secker and Warburg.

Brookes, M. (2004) *Watching Alone: Social capital and public service broadcasting.* London: The Work Foundation in partnership with the BBC.

Cave, M. (2004) *Competition in broadcasting – consequences for viewers.* Research paper prepared for Ofcom.

Cox, B. (2004) *Free for All? Public Service Television in the Digital Age.* London: Demos

Davies, G. *et al* (1999) *The Future Funding of the BBC: Report of the Independent Review Panel.* London: Department of Culture, Media and Sport

Ehrenberg, A. and P. Mills (1990) *Viewers Willingness to Pay: A Research Report.* London: International Thompson Business Publishing.

Elstein *et al* (2004) *Beyond the Charter: The BBC after 2006*. Report of the Broadcasting Policy Group. London: Premium Publishing

Graham, A. and G. Davies (1990) *Why Private Choice Needs Public Broadcasting*. London: Royal Television Society.

Graham, A. and G. Davies (1992) 'The Public Funding of Broadcasting' in T. Congdon (ed.) *Paying for Broadcasting*. London: Routledge.

Graham, A. and G. Davies (1997) *Broadcasting, Society and Policy in the Multimedia Age*. John Libbey Media, University of Luton

Hamilton, J.T. (1998) *Channeling Violence: The Economic Market for Violent Television Programming*. Princeton University Press.

Hirschman, A. (1982) *Shifting Involvements: Private Interest and Public Action*. Princeton University Press, reprinted in 1985 by Basil Blackwell Ltd, Oxford.

Independent Television Commission (ITC) (2001) *Culture and Communications: perspectives on broadcasting and the information society*. London: Independent Television Commission.

Ofcom (2004a) *Ofcom review of public service broadcasting, Phase 1 – Is television special?* London: Office of Communications.

Ofcom (2004b) *Ofcom review of public service broadcasting, Phase 2 – Meeting the digital challenge*. London: Office of Communications.

Ofcom (2004c) *Valuing PSB: the view from the audience*. London: Office of Communications.

Peacock *et al*. *Report of the Committee on Financing the BBC*. London: HMSO, 1986.

Schlesinger, P. (2004) *Do Institutions Matter for Public Service Broadcasting?* Research paper prepared for Ofcom.

Woodrow, W. (1999) 'Journal for 1 December 1995', *The Journals of Woodrow Wyatt: Volume One*. Pan

6

Paying for Public Service Television in the Digital Age

Bill Robinson, John Raven and Lit Ping Low

1. Introduction and overview

The distribution revolution

The arrival of satellite and cable distribution systems has massively increased the number of television channels in the UK. The use of digital transmission technology has amplified the effect. This technological revolution in television distribution has weakened two important economic arguments for Public Service Broadcasting (PSB). Firstly, because the number of broadcasting channels is no longer limited, there is no need for public intervention to ensure that niche interests are catered for. And, secondly, because broadcasting has become excludable, a market can in principle develop to cater for all tastes as people are given the opportunity to buy the programmes (or bundles of programmes) that they prefer. In addition, the distribution revolution has made it harder to impose PSB obligations on the terrestrial commercial broadcasters because the rent they used to enjoy when spectrum was scarce has now been eroded by the activities of the new commercial channels.

The role of Public Service Broadcasting in a multi-channel world

These changes have prompted a radical re-think of the case for PSB, which must now rest on the desire to create and broadcast programmes that the market would not supply on its own. The recent Ofcom review concluded that PSB programmes should be defined by their *purposes* (to inform, to educate, to define our cultural identity while making us aware of other cultures) and by their *characteristics* (universally available, well-funded and well produced, innovative, challenging, and distinctively British).

The commercial market can be expected to supply less programming of this sort than is socially optimal because broadcasting, though now excludable, is still non-rival. One person's enjoyment of television programmes does not impair another's, so that additional viewers can be reached at zero marginal cost. The distribution revolution has made it *possible* for pay-TV to replace licence fee funding. It does not follow that this is *desirable*.

The influence of funding on programmes

Whether or not it is desirable depends on whether more PSB programmes would be made in a world in which licence-funding existed alongside other commercial funding methods. The many funding methods can be divided into two main categories: those based on the willingness of (a) viewers to pay for content; and (b) advertisers to pay to transmit advertisements.

The method of funding clearly influences the kind of programme the broadcaster makes. Advertisers are primarily concerned that many people *see the commercials*, not with how much they *enjoy the programmes*. So the aim of advertising-funded channels is to maximise audiences and minimise programming costs. Subscription channels on the other hand have to supply a schedule of programmes which are *sufficiently valued* to justify renewing the subscriptions – just as the BBC has to deliver a schedule which justifies the licence fee.

Both the BBC and the subscription channels face incentives very different from pay-per-view, where each *programme* has to deliver sufficient revenue to justify its cost. In some respects the BBC is like a subscription channel, with the unusual characteristics that the subscription (licence fee) is (a) compulsory to all owners of television sets and (b) justified in part by meeting PSB objectives. The benefit of compulsion is that the BBC has a universal reach and is therefore relatively cheap. The cost is that viewers who do not value BBC programmes are burdened with a licence fee that they regard as an unnecessary tax.

How the television market has developed

When encryption arrived, many expected that television broadcasts, like films, would be increasingly sold in a market in which viewers paid directly for programmes that appealed to them. It was expected that pay per view, and niche channels, would flourish. More than a decade later it is clear this has not happened to the extent many predicted. There are some viable channels providing children's programmes, news and documentaries. But they account for a tiny proportion of total viewing and overall programme investment.

The main impact of the distribution revolution is that new broad-appeal commercial channels have emerged to challenge the ITV hegemony. In general they offer a mix of programmes with a heavy emphasis on imported American programming, recent-release films and sports. But the new subscription channels have not in practice challenged the BBC's role as a provider of serious PSB programming even though in theory they might.

How should the BBC be funded?

This establishes a strong case for allowing the BBC to continue as a key PSB provider, but it leaves open the question as to how it should be funded. If PSB can in principle be supplied by subscription channels, why not turn the BBC into a subscription service thus preserving a PSB champion, with a strong tradition of PSB provision, at no cost to public funds? The strongest argument for moving to a subscription-funded BBC is the welfare loss of compulsion. Those who do *not* want to watch the BBC are obliged to pay an unpopular tax on television set ownership in order to reach the channels that they *do* want to watch.

New research on the willingness to pay for the BBC enables us to draw a demand curve for BBC services and calculate the welfare gains and losses of moving from a compulsory licence fee to a voluntary subscription service. We find that the welfare losses from those who are required to pay more for their viewing, or who are excluded altogether, outweigh the gains to those who are liberated from a compulsory licence. In addition we find that the profit-maximising subscription revenue is less than licence fee revenue, implying a reduction in quality of PSB programming. Moreover, the BBC would be watched by only 14 million of the 24.5 million television households and would cease to be a universal service.

2. Public Service Broadcasting

History

When television broadcasting recommenced in 1947 the 'commanding heights' of the British economy had just been nationalised. Broadcasting technology was limited to free-to-air distribution. Under those circumstances it was natural that the relaunch of television would be placed in the hands of a public provider. The BBC (which still inspired huge public affection as the wartime voice of Britain), was given a remit to reach everyone and to provide, on a single channel, a mix of programmes that satisfied all tastes. These were the key objectives of PSB in the early post-war period.

When a second, commercial, channel was launched in 1955, the ITV companies were granted access to scarce spectrum on condition that they also rolled out the service to all parts of the United Kingdom and committed to supplying a balanced mix of programming to suit all tastes. The immense value of the scarce spectrum made it easy to impose these additional costs on the ITV companies. The second channel was also broadcast free to air and funded by advertising. Access to the spectrum enabled the companies to generate advertising revenues well above the cost of providing programmes. The first commercial licence, even though surrounded by restrictions on broadcasters' freedom, was famously described as a 'licence to print money'.

From 1955 to the early 1990s, the television industry enjoyed steady growth of revenues, driven first by the penetration of television itself, and subsequently by the spread of colour television, launched in 1969. Colour boosted both licence revenues (because the colour licence was more expensive) and advertising revenues (because colour greatly enhanced the power of the medium and attracted a wider range of advertisers).

But despite the huge success and great profitability of television, spectrum scarcity remained an insuperable barrier to entry. No new broadcasters entered this rapidly growing market until Channel 4 was formally created by an Act of Parliament in 1982. Even when the fifth terrestrial channel, Five (formerly Channel 5) was launched in 1997, the lack of spectrum space meant that many areas were unable to receive its transmission via analogue terrestrial broadcasts.

The entry barriers came down in the early 1990s following a technological revolution in the distribution of television programmes. The system of terrestrial distribution by a network of masts designed to deliver television as a universal public service (i.e. reaching every home in the land) was supplemented by cable and satellite networks rolled out on a commercial basis. The landmark event was the launch in 1990 of BSkyB (formed by a merger between Sky Television and British Satellite Broadcasting) which broke the mould in two important respects:

- The terrestrial distribution system was no longer the single gateway to viewers;

- The new distribution channels made no attempt to reach all the people; they aimed to roll out the service to as many people as could be reached on commercially viable terms and hence deliver a large audience to be exploited for commercial purposes.

The subsequent spread of digital television technology increased the carrying capacity of all channels, expanding the number of channels on the terrestrial network (digital terrestrial television) as well as on the new satellite and cable networks.

The distribution revolution meant that the public sector no longer controlled access to the airwaves. The monopoly of distribution was effectively broken, at least in large population centres and in homes reachable by satellite. A further important feature of the new distribution technologies was that programmes could, for the first time, be transmitted on a conditional access basis, and received only by those who were willing to pay.

These changes have weakened two commonly-used economic arguments for public service broadcasting by a publicly owned broadcaster such as the BBC. Firstly, because the number of broadcasting channels is no longer limited, there is less need for public intervention to ensure that niche interests are catered for. And, secondly, because broadcasting has become excludable, a market can in principle develop to cater for all tastes as people are given the opportunity to buy the programmes (or bundles of programmes) that they prefer.

The distribution revolution has also affected the case for imposing PSB obligations on commercial broadcasters. The emergence of new commercial channels focussing on audience-pleasing popular programming posed a particular threat to the traditional advertising funded channels. It reduced their audience share and consequently reduced the growth of advertising revenue, gradually eliminating the economic rent enjoyed by the commercial channels in the days of spectrum scarcity. That rent made it possible to attach PSB conditions to the award of licences. The imposition of such conditions will become increasingly difficult in the digital age. The commercial broadcasters also claim it is unnecessary, because all tastes can now be catered for commercially.

What is meant by PSB?

These changes have made it necessary to redefine public service broadcasting. In the early days the licence fee was effectively the only method of funding on offer. When advertising funded television was launched, the licence fee remained the only way of paying for programmes that appealed only to certain special interest groups. Now that there is a large variety of channels and of funding methods, the case for licence fee funded public service broadcasting needs re-thinking. It must rest on the need to create and transmit certain kinds of programmes that the market would not otherwise supply.

As Ofcom neatly puts it, public service broadcasting in the UK as defined by the Communications Act 2003 should include programmes and services which, taken together, meet the following criteria:

- *Range and balance* – the programming schedule should cover a range of different types of programming, with a balanced pattern of investment on different genres;

- *Diversity* – programming should be targeted at different audience types, and should represent different viewpoints;

- *Quality* – achieving excellence in programming, including high production values, originality and innovation, ambition and risk-taking; and

- *Social values* – the wider benefits of television to society, including cultural identity (e.g. reflection of different parts of the UK), informed democracy (e.g. impartial news and current affairs) and educated citizens (including educational and children's programming, as well as informative factual programming).

More recently, the Phase 2 report of the Ofcom PSTB review argued that broadcasting should in the digital future be defined in terms of *purposes* and *characteristics* rather than types of programmes or output. They have suggested that these purposes should be:

- To *inform and increase understanding* of the world through news, information and analysis of current events and ideas;

- To stimulate interest in and knowledge of *arts, science, history and other topics* through content that is accessible and can encourage informal learning;

- To reflect and strengthen *cultural identity through original programming* at UK, national and regional level; and

- To increase awareness *of different cultures and alternative viewpoints* both within the UK and elsewhere.

and the characteristics should be:

- *High quality* – well-funded and well-produced;

- *Original* – new UK content;

- *Innovative* – new ideas or re-inventing exciting approaches;

- *Challenging* – make viewers think;

- *Engaging* – remain accessible and enjoyable to watch; and

- *Widely available* – publicly funded content should be available to the large majority of citizens.[1]

Arguments for public provision of PSB

The above descriptions from the Communications Act and Ofcom summarise the objectives of public service broadcasting. But how are these objectives different from those of a private broadcaster? Why might not a private broadcaster deliver these objectives?

Excludability

Before the distribution revolution there was a very simple answer to this question. Broadcasting could only take place free to air. Broadcasters could not charge viewers to see their programmes. So private broadcasters had no source of revenue other than advertising revenue. Since advertising revenue depended on producing popular programmes intended to maximise the sheer number of viewers, privately funded broadcasters had no incentive to cater to niche interests. Intervention was needed to achieve PSB objectives.

In economic terms, broadcasting was a classic example of a public good. Public goods (light houses are the text book example) are likely to be under-supplied by the private sector, because they are 'non-excludable'. This means that once they are produced, it is impossible to exclude people from consuming the good – and therefore impossible for a private firm to charge for the good. Broadcasting used to be like this. But clearly this situation has changed with conditional access. Private provision is now possible. The question is whether it is socially optimal.

Non-rivalry

An important reason why it might not be socially optimal is based on another public good characteristic of broadcasting: non-rivalry. This means that the consumption of the good by one person does not decrease the amount available for everyone else. The marginal cost of an extra viewer is zero, so the socially optimal price for viewing is zero. The fact that you now *can* charge for broadcasting does not necessarily mean that you *should*. Charging excludes

---

1   (Ofcom 2004b) *Ofcom Review of Public Service Television Broadcasting: Phase 2 – Meeting the Digital Challenge*, p. 110.

those who cannot afford the charge and there is a welfare loss from this exclusion which is avoided by funding methods based on free-to-air access.

Externalities

Another well-known economic argument for PSB is based on the spill-over effects of television broadcasting on social behaviour. 'Good' broadcasting can encourage behaviour that is beneficial to society at large while 'bad' broadcasting may encourage behaviour that is detrimental to society. But if 'bad' programmes (e.g. which glamourise violence) are more profitable than 'good' programmes (e.g. educational programmes which make us better citizens), the private sector will produce too many 'bad' and too few 'good' programmes. Intervention is justified to produce a balance that is socially optimal.

The advent of subscription funded conditional access broadcasting may increase the commercial incentives to make 'bad' programmes. So arguably there is a greater *need*, following the distribution revolution, both for regulation, to restrict the output of 'bad' programmes, and for PSB, to increase the output of 'good' programmes. On the other hand the proliferation of channels means that the *effectiveness* of positive intervention will be much more limited than in the past. Those who prefer to watch 'bad' programmes will find plenty available in the multi-channel world.

Merit goods

Merit goods are goods (such as fresh fruit, or healthcare) the consumption of which is beneficial rather than enjoyable, so that people consume less than is good for them. Some broadcasting comes into this category and there is a case for intervention to increase the output of programmes such as news and documentaries. This feature of broadcasting is precisely what is identified by Ofcom as one of the purposes of PSB.

However with merit goods, as with externalities, the problem is not that the *case* for intervention has been weakened. The distribution revolution does not eliminate these kinds of market failure. But it has hugely reduced the *effectiveness* of intervention to deal with them. The multiplicity of channels means that although PSB can still be supplied, the chances of it being watched are much reduced. It has become much harder to get viewers to watch programmes that are deemed to be 'good' – either for the viewer himself or for society as a whole.

In summary, although broadcasting has lost one of its public good characteristics, being now *excludable*, the case for PSB intervention based on the *non-rival* nature of broadcasting is as strong as ever. Once a programme is on the air, extra viewers can be served at zero marginal cost, and the participation of these additional viewers does not diminish the enjoyment of existing viewers. Indeed, it arguably enhances it, through the pleasure of shared experience of popular television programmes. Our analysis also suggests that the economic case for intervention to increase the supply of PSB programming is unchanged. What has changed is the effectiveness of PSB intervention in a world in which viewers have a wide choice of other programmes to watch.

3. The influence of funding on what programmes are broadcast

Alternative funding methods

The new feature of the broadcasting ecology, since the distribution revolution, is the existence of subscription services. The interesting question is whether subscription services could be relied upon to supply PSB programming, or whether they would undersupply such programming. This depends on the incentives placed on broadcasters under different funding methods.

Broadcasters around the world depend on a wide variety of different sources of revenue: government grants, licence fee, advertising, sponsorship, royalties from programme sales, publishing and merchandise spin-offs, subscriptions and pay-per-view. But two broad categories dominate:

1. The state pays the broadcaster to create and transmit programmes, which are transmitted free to air. The method of payment can be a direct grant, paid from general tax receipts, or a compulsory licence fee, sometimes described as a hypothecated tax.

2. Advertisers pay broadcasters for the right to insert commercials into programmes, which are transmitted free to air. This category embraces sponsorship of programmes as well as the more common practice of advertising in the commercial breaks between or within programmes.

Encryption has made possible a third option:

3. Viewers pay broadcasters for the right to watch programmes, by buying a subscription to a bundle of channels, a subscription to a single channel, or a one-off payment to watch a single programme (pay-per-view).

The market for television has as a result become more like the market for newspapers. The cost of production is borne in part by selling advertising and in part by direct payments for content (cf. the cover price of a newspaper). But encryption has not, by and large, created a market for individual *programmes*. Pay per view is limited to some major sporting events (mainly boxing matches) and recently-released films. Television is typically sold as a subscription service for a channel or a bundle of channels.

This fact blurs the distinction between the licence-fee funded BBC and the commercial subscription services. The BBC is often regarded as a pure PSB broadcaster. But it can also be argued that the BBC is a subscription service with the unusual characteristic that the subscription is compulsory and accompanied by obligations to transmit certain kinds of programme. This element of compulsion does not insulate the BBC from the pressure to satisfy its audiences, because the licence is regularly reviewed and has to be politically justified. Compulsion means that the BBC both has a universal reach and is significantly cheaper than its subscription-funded competitors. It also means that those who do not value the BBC, but are obliged to buy television licences, regard the licence fee as a pure tax.

Who makes what programmes?[2]

It does not matter what label we apply to any particular funding method. What does matter are the pressures put on broadcasters, under different funding methods, to make different kinds of programmes. There is a wide variety of programmes on television and they are valued in different ways. There are two key variables: the number of people who watch; and the value each of them places on the programme. It is worth distinguishing between three kinds of programme:

- Wide appeal, low value per viewer

- Narrow appeal, high value per viewer

- Wide appeal, mixed value per viewer (i.e. different viewers attach very different values to the programme)

We discuss each, with examples, below:

- *Wide appeal, low value:* Some programmes, such as a game show, may appeal to a very wide audience. It keeps them watching, but if you asked them after the event how much they had enjoyed it, or how much they

2   Christian Koboldt et al, 'The Implications of Funding for Broadcasting Output' in *Public Purposes in Broadcasting: Funding the BBC*, 1999.

would pay to watch it if it were only available on pay per view, many would attach a relatively low value. Clearly a programme of this sort would be attractive to advertisers, whose primary concern is the number of people who see their commercials.

- *Narrow appeal, high value:* Other programmes, a minority sport like rugby, or a minority taste such as opera or French cinema, may attract a relatively small audience but each viewer would attach a very high value to the programme. Such a programme would be a natural for a specialist channel, or for pay-per-view. The reason is that the total value of such programmes, to those who like them, is high, and the value can be captured by a direct payment mechanism.

- *Wide appeal, mixed value:* The third kind of programme might be a prestige programme, which we will assume is expensive to produce, such as a major sporting event, a much-loved soap or a costume drama. Such programmes typically attract large audiences. Some of the viewers may value the programme enormously. But others may place quite a low value on the programme. The total value may be a large sum which would cover the large cost of the programme. A publicly funded broadcaster would not hesitate to produce such a programme. But if the programme had to be sold commercially, it could well prove unviable. Although the audience is large, making the programme attractive to advertisers, it may not be larger than the audience for a much cheaper game show. For advertiser funded channels, such programmes are unlikely to be the most cost effective way of delivering audiences, though they may well have the benefit of extending reach and differentiating the channels. If the programme is sold on a pay per view basis, there is a more fundamental problem. If the price is set high to capture the value that the enthusiasts attach to the programme, the audience will be very small. If it is set low to pull in the audience, then the high value attached to the programme by the enthusiast will not be captured.

Welfare maximisation vs. revenue maximisation

The above example suggests that there are certain kinds of programme that are most likely to be made by public service broadcasters – though as we shall show below, some subscription channels could in principle make them. Figure 1 shows a typical downward sloping demand curve for the programme in question. The area under the curve represents the total value placed on the programme. If a

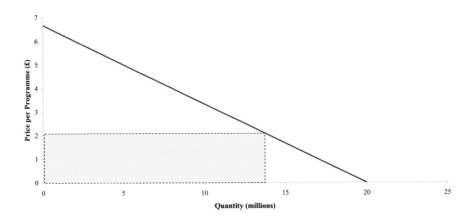

Figure 1. Demand curve for a single programme.

perfectly discriminating monopolist could charge each viewer exactly what he was willing to pay, this is the amount of revenue he would extract. But the normal commercial reality is that a single price is set and the revenue is the rectangle showing the quantity sold multiplied by the price charged. It is clear from Figure 1 that the area of the rectangle is much smaller than the area under the curve.

Suppose now that the cost of the programme is greater than the rectangle but smaller than the area under the curve. Under a pay per view or advertising funding mechanism the programme is much less likely to be made than under a public funding mechanism. The broadcaster will transmit the programme free to air, knowing that everybody who values it at all will watch it. So the total value as perceived by the viewers of that transmission is the area under the curve. Since the remit of the PSB broadcaster is to deliver the maximum value to the maximum number of viewers, the programme is worth making and transmitting.

In summary, as Table 1 shows, if a programme guarantees a large audience of people who each value it highly, it would be attractive to any broadcaster, whatever the funding method. A programme with a small audience, each of whom valued it little is a programme that no broadcaster would make. Programmes attracting large audiences each of whom places a relatively low value on the programme are likely to be made by advertising funded broadcasters, whose main concern is that people watch, not that they enjoy. Programmes attracting small audiences of enthusiasts would seem to be a natural for pay per view or specialist subscription channels.

Table 1: Audience vs. value per viewer

Size of audience	Value per viewer		
	High	**Mixed**	**Low**
Large	All	PSB or general subscription channel	Advertising
Small	Pay per view or specialist subscription channel	PSB or general subscription channel	None

But programmes which generate a mixed reaction from the audience will suffer from the problem that their full value can never be captured on the pay-per-view model. Such programmes will only be made by a broadcaster who justifies charging for a bundle of programmes on the basis of the total value delivered by that bundle. In the past that has been the public service broadcasters. In principle, as we shall show, subscription services may also have an incentive to supply mixed-value programmes as part of their schedules.

Subscription channels – the bundling of programmes

When encryption became possible, many expected it to lead to a market in television programmes. The reality is that the purchase of individual programmes by viewers is a comparatively rare event – only very new films and a few major sporting events are sold in this way. Generally, television programmes are sold to audiences only after they have been bundled into channels. Broadcasters can bundle groups of programmes, either of the same or different genres, into a channel. The channel can then either be 'sold' individually, or bundled with other channels, again either the same or different genres, to be sold as a package of channels.

How do broadcasters running commercial subscription channels decide what programmes should be made and broadcast on their channels? Their chief concern is to maximise the revenues from, and minimise the costs of the bundle of programmes which make up the channel. Bundling is a well-known commercial technique for extracting value. It is particularly effective in the broadcasting market where the marginal costs of distributing programmes are very low relative to their potential value to viewers. Adding a new programme to a bundle of programmes typically increases value to the viewer, and hence revenue, more than it increases costs. Consumers appreciate having a variety of programmes on the same channel, particularly if they do not have many other channels to switch to, and possibly even if they do[3].

113

For a subscription funded broadcaster what matters is the *ex post* perception of the value of the channel. Thus, while it may be expensive to commission costume dramas, a subscription channel may decide to incur this expense. Even if the programme itself does not attract any more viewers than a much cheaper game show, the value that it adds to the whole channel may still make it a commercially sensible venture. There may even be some costume-drama enthusiasts for whom this programme alone almost justifies the subscription to the channel.

The power of bundling as a revenue and utility maximising device is illustrated by Table 2 which shows a very simplified world with only two programmes and two viewers.

Table 2: Why bundling dominates pay per view

	Value to Viewer	Price	Revenue	Utility
Programme A		5		
Viewer 1 (a₁)	5		5	5
Viewer 2 (a₂)	2		0	0
Programme B2		2		
Viewer 1 (b₁)	2		2	2
Viewer 2 (b₂)	3		2	3
Total			9	10
Bundle A+B5		5		
Viewer 1 (a₁ + b₁)	7		5	7
Viewer 2 (a₂ + b₂)	5		5	5
Total			10	12

Programme A (the highly but narrowly valued niche programme) has a huge appeal for Viewer 1, but much less for Viewer 2. Programme B (the wide appeal programme) appeals to both viewers, but more to Viewer 2. If the two programmes are provided individually on a pay-per-view basis, the optimal strategy would be to provide:

- Programme A at a price of 5. Only Viewer 1 will buy it at that price so revenue is 5. The alternative is to charge a price of 2, to pull in Viewer 2. But at that price total revenue is only 4. The optimal commercial pricing strategy thus delivers 5 units of revenue and 5 units of social utility; and

- Programme B at a price of 2 to both Viewers 1 and 2, producing 4 units of revenue and 5 units of social utility. For the programme with broad and

3 Professor Patrick Barwise, *Independent Review of the BBC's Digital Television Services*, 2004.

shallow appeal it is worth setting the price low enough to bring in both viewers. The alternative, of attempting to extract more value from those who value the programme highly, is to charge 3, which produces revenue of only 3. The optimal strategy thus delivers 4 units of revenue and 5 units of social utility.

To sum up, the strategy of selling the programmes individually can at best produce 9 units of revenue and 10 units of social utility.

However, if the broadcaster offered a subscription channel, providing both Programmes A and B, the optimal strategy would be to charge a *subscription* price of 5. This would attract both Viewers 1 and 2 because the sum of the value of the two programmes is 7 for Viewer 1 and 5 for Viewer 2. The bundling strategy would produce 10 units of revenue – higher than the sum of the revenues produced on a pay-per-view basis. It would also produce more social utility, totalling 12 units, as both viewers would watch both programmes. The bundling strategy would thus be superior, as it can extract more value by supplying a variety of programmes, and viewers would not be excluded.

This analysis explains why subscription funding methods (including the licence fee) dominate pay per view when the audiences have mixed valuations of programmes. In a pay-per-view world the broadcaster's profit maximising price will exclude many viewers who place a value on the programme which is less than the profit maximising pay-per-view price. They do not see the programme (which is socially sub-optimal) and the money they would be prepared to pay to watch the programme is not captured by the broadcaster (which is commercially sub-optimal). By contrast in the subscription world the lesser value that those viewers place on the programme contributes to their willingness to pay the subscription price (which is why subscription works commercially). And once the subscription is paid, all programmes are essentially free at the margin. More programmes therefore get watched, which is why bundling delivers more social value.

This analysis suggests that, unlike advertising funded broadcasters, who are bound to concentrate on mass appeal programmes in order to maximise audiences, subscription channels have an incentive to provide some niche programmes, because their value is captured by increasing the willingness of the minorities who enjoy those programmes to pay the subscription.

Extending this argument to the bundling of channels, larger broadcasters will have the incentives to create niche channels, and funding them either by pay-per-view or as part of a larger bundle. A subscription broadcaster who could only produce one channel may wish to choose a genre with wide appeal and/or high value, but the ability to sell packages of channels means that the broadcaster can produce several channels with different target audiences.

If these arguments suggest that subscription funded broadcasters might behave in ways that are very similar to a public service broadcaster, such as the BBC, that should be no surprise. The BBC is in effect a subscription-funded broadcaster, which is ever mindful of the need to justify the licence fee. However, as the next section will show, subscription channels have not exhibited signs of replacing the functions of the PSB channels, and seem unlikely to do so in the near future. The empirical evidence would not appear to support the theoretical arguments for the potential efficiency of subscription channels as PSB providers.

4. The changing structure of television broadcasting in the UK

The market for television

Television is a very significant recreational activity in the UK. The average person spends 2.5 hours watching television and video per day, significantly more than any other leisure activity. Television is the third highest component of the average weekly expenditure at £7 on 'recreation and culture', after 'holidays' and 'equipments' and 'durables'. Over 80 per cent of households now own more than one TV set, up from 75 per cent in 1998 and 32 per cent in 1980.

Multi-channel and digital take-up

Table 3 compares the main changes in television broadcasting in the last five years. The new channels (including Five) have increased audience share at the expense of traditional channels, with the biggest increase by far accruing to the non-terrestrial channels.

Table 3: Comparison between 1998 and 2003 – penetration and viewing shares

Penetration (million)	1998	2003
Multi-channel homes	7.1	14.6*
Digital homes	0.4	13.7*
Viewing Shares (%)		
BBC One	29.5	25.6
BBC Two	11.3	11.0
ITV	31.7	23.7
Channel 4	10.3	9.6
Five	4.3	6.5
Multi-channels	12.9	23.6

*Q2 figures.

The distribution revolution has led to a sharp rise in multi-channel households,

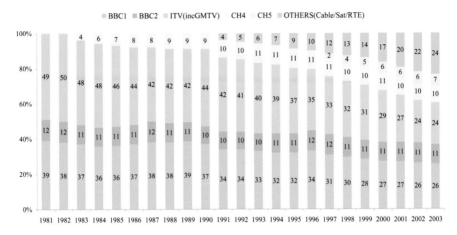

Figure 2. Viewing Shares of Channels 1981–2003. [Source: BARB.]

from 7 million or 29 per cent of households in 1998 to over half of all households in 2004. The number of digital homes has risen even more sharply as satellite broadcasters have successfully moved onto a digital platform, with cable progressing in the same direction. The number of households taking up digital terrestrial television (DTT) is on a rapidly accelerating curve as the Freeview box gains increasingly widespread acceptance.

The growing multi channel penetration reflects the falling costs of digital and multi-channel subscription packages. In particular free-to-air DTT penetration has almost doubled in the last year alone because of the success of the Freeview package, accessed via a cheap set-top box for a one-off £50 charge. The bundling of digital and cable television subscription services and equipment with internet, telephone services and television sets is another form of cost reduction which will contribute to further growth in digital penetration.

Audience shares

The rise of multi-channel distribution has resulted in a substantial increase in the number of channels available, now well over 300. Although the viewing share of the main terrestrial channels (BBC One, BBC Two, ITV1, Channel 4 and recently Five) has fallen in the past decade, these channels still account for around three quarters of total viewing as Figure 2 shows.

Since 1998 the new channels, including Five, have between them taken 13 per cent of the market, of which 8 percentage points have come from ITV1 and 4 from BBC One. The new entrants have thus grown at the expense of the

117

mass-audience channels, especially ITV1. The more serious channels, BBC Two and Channel 4, which arguably contain a higher proportion of programming which meets PSB objectives, have maintained market share.

The new channels are individually small. The largest, Sky One, takes less than 3 per cent of viewing. This is less than half the share of newest terrestrial channel, Five, even though it has been going twice as long – testimony to the enduring attraction of free television. Collectively the new channels have achieved a 24 per cent viewing share with a very large number of channels each attracting a tiny market share.

Genre viewing in multi-channel homes

The proportion of viewing times on the traditional PSB-focused genres (news, children's, current affairs and general factual) is lower in multi-channel homes. For example, in 2002, 34 per cent of the viewing of 16–34 year olds on terrestrial television was dedicated to the abovementioned genres, whereas the equivalent of this on the multi-channel homes was 29 per cent[4]. A possible explanation is that viewers who are less interested in these genres migrate to the multi-channel world in search of more entertainment. There is also a striking fall in the share of drama (27 per cent on terrestrial vs. 15 per cent on multi-channel for the 16–34 age group), which may be because the new channels have yet to make programmes which match the pulling power of soaps such as *Coronation Street* or *EastEnders*.

Impact on Channel 3 advertising revenue

The decline in audience share of the terrestrial channels has had a serious impact on their advertising revenues as Table 4 shows. The advent of competition from the multi-channel broadcasters, all of whom offer advertising slots and collectively can reach significant audiences, has dramatically slowed the growth of terrestrial advertising revenues. Over the period 1975–91, from trough to trough of the economic cycle, terrestrial advertising revenues grew by 6 per cent per annum in real terms. The average real rate of growth since 1991 is 1 per cent. The position of ITV, which was by far the biggest channel, is considerably worse than this, since it has also suffered from competition from Five. These statistics show how the distribution revolution has eroded the economic rent formerly enjoyed by terrestrial commercial licence holders. Some of that rent

4   Source: Ofcom, *Review of Public Service Television Broadcasting, Phase 1: Is Television Special*, 2004.

was used, under the conditions on which licences were awarded, to fund the
output of PSB programming by commercial broadcasters.

Table 4: Growth of advertising revenue

Average annual growth rates of advertising revenue (%)	1975–1991	1991–2003
Commercial terrestrial channels	6%	1%
Multi-channels	n.a.	24%
Total TV	6%	3%

PSB in a multi-channel world

Fourteen years after the arrival of satellite television perhaps the most striking
feature of the television market is the continued dominance of the five main
terrestrial channels. The new entrants into the television market have taken most
market share from the advertising funded ITV. This is hardly surprising. New
commercially-motivated broadcasters have targeted the commercial end of the
television market with a programme mix that most resembles the ITV offering.
The rise of multi-channel television has clearly resulted in a greater availability
of non-PSB programming, and a significant proportion of the viewing
population has migrated to the multi-channel world in order to increase its
viewing of the pure entertainment genres. The other side of this is the
remarkable stability of the viewing share of Channel 4 and BBC Two. Again this
should not surprise us. Those who enjoyed mass-appeal television programmes
have been attracted by the multi-channel offerings. Those who prefer PSB
programmes have not.

The hope that multi-channel television would deliver variety and quality in the
form of niche channels providing high-value programmes to small group of
audiences has been only partly realised. Sports enthusiasts are much better
served than before. There are more specialist children's channels. There is a
greater variety of more recent films available.

Table 5: Television revenues

Year	BBC		Commercial terrestrial channels		Multi-channels		Total TV	
	2003	1993	2003	1993	2003	1993	2003	1993
Total revenue (£ million)	2681	1800*	2637	1813	3186	380	8504	3993
%of total	32	45	31	45	37	20	100	100

*Estimated.

However, the multi-channel world, which accounts for 24 per cent of audiences and 37 per cent of total television revenues (see Table 5), accounts for a much smaller proportion of UK-originated programme spend (excluding sports). The new money that has come into the industry as a result of the distribution revolution has offered viewers more variety and choice, but it has not led to the creation of new television programmes on any significant scale. A recent study has revealed that pay television channels in the UK spend only £100 million on new UK programming, compared with BBC's £1,100 million.[5] The obvious explanation is that, as a result of PSB obligations mandating a high proportion of UK content in the terrestrial channels, there was in the UK an unsatisfied demand for American television programmes and sport. US programmes and sports could be bought, and broadcast on the new channels, to deliver a relatively predictable profit. A commercial strategy based on US imports thus made a lot more sense than the riskier strategy of challenging the incumbents on their home ground – the provision of UK-originated programmes.

The BBC (and ITV to a certain extent) have always had both the capability and incentive to produce relatively high-cost, high-quality UK content. One of the incentives was their PSB obligations. But it is also noticeable that ITV has responded to the challenge from the new commercial channels by building its schedules around quality UK drama. Thus both BBC and ITV have built up large audiences who expect and value good UK-originated material. They have teams of writers and producers and commissioning editors with the expertise to deliver such programmes. So it is much easier for the incumbents to go on delivering this kind of programme than it is for the new entrants to break into the market.

For these reasons, pay television channels in the UK have not delivered PSB programming, and are unlikely to do so for the foreseeable future. This is in contrast to the situation in the US where the commercial market has delivered a number of programmes (e.g. *The West Wing*) which clearly meet PSB standards. Why has no equivalent of HBO, a large pay-TV broadcaster in the US, which produces significant amount of high-quality programmes, sprung up in the UK pay television market?

There are two important differences between the UK and the US which explain this. The first, as mentioned above, is that there is no strong licence fee funded PSB supplier in the US, so there is a gap in the market which HBO had a commercial incentive to fill. The second is that the US market is five times bigger than the UK.[6] So even a small part of this enormous market provides a target

---

5   Oliver & Ohlbaum Associates Ltd, *UK Television Content in the Digital Age*, 2003.

audience of sufficient size and wealth to justify the large risks of providing up-market originated programming. The fact that HBO flourishes in the commercial US market, which is very large and lacks a licence fee funded PSB provider, does not mean that a similar channel might spring up in the UK pay television market, a much smaller market with a strong tradition of relatively up-market programme provision by incumbent free-to-air broadcasters.

5. Funding options

The Funding of the BBC

In Section 3 we argued that subscription channels could in principle be expected to deliver PSB. Section 4 has shown that in practice they have shown little sign of doing so for good strategic commercial reasons. Section 4 has also underlined the massive erosion of market share, and hence advertising revenues, suffered by ITV1 as a result of the distribution revolution. The licence to broadcast on Channel 3 is no longer a 'licence to print money', and increasingly it can no longer be hedged with PSB conditions. This leaves the BBC as the main potential provider of PSB. But given that the BBC is in many respects very similar to a subscription service, we can ask why the BBC should be funded by a compulsory licence fee rather than by subscriptions.

A subscription-funded BBC would be an attractive free-market solution to the problem of broadcasting funding. It would finally end the perennial debate about the proper size of the licence fee. It would give complete independence to a powerful broadcaster with a strong tradition of PSB programming. It would eliminate the problem of levying licence fees, often described as a regressive tax on television ownership, from the poorer members of society. But these advantages must be balanced against two major disadvantages:

- a subscription funded BBC would have to charge more than the present licence fee to finance its operations; and

- those who do not subscribe would be totally excluded from viewing BBC programmes, invalidating one of the major aims of PSB which is universality.

Compared with subscription funding, the licence fee has one obvious disadvantage, namely compulsion. It has two great advantages: cheapness and

6   Mediatique Ltd, *A Consideration of Aspects of the Pay-TV Market in the UK in the Absence of Public Service Obligations*, August 2004.

universal reach. Given a demand curve for BBC services it is relatively simple to calculate the welfare loss due to compulsion and compare it with the welfare gains which result from a cheaper service watched by more people. Thanks to an interesting new study of willingness to pay for BBC services, recently carried out by the BBC and Human Capital (see Chapter 4),[7] we can, by making a number of assumptions, calculate the welfare gains and losses resulting from adopting licence funding rather than subscription funding. We have calculated these gains and losses based on our own assumptions. Our results are similar to those calculated by Human Capital under slightly different assumptions.

Licence-funded BBC

The BBC and Human Capital study tells us how many people would be willing to buy BBC services at different prices ranging at £10 intervals from £60 to £20 and at £5 intervals down to £5. Each of these observations is a point on the demand curve for the BBC, showing how many would subscribe at a given price. By joining up these points we can draw a classic demand curve for BBC services, as shown in Table 3.

There are 25 million homes in the UK, of which 24.5 million households pay the licence fee, generating £2.66 billion annually for the BBC. A significant proportion of households (up to 5 million) think that BBC services are worth less to them (as consumers) than the licence fee, but a large majority of households are willing to pay more. The total value of the BBC is given by the area under the curve, which we calculate at £5.43 billion annually. The difference between this value and the cost of the licence fee is a consumer surplus worth £(5.43 − 2.66) = 2.77 billion.

However, there are those who buy the licence mainly in order to watch non-BBC channels. The value of BBC programmes to these viewers is less than £10 per month. This group of households effectively suffers a loss of welfare due to the mandatory licence fee. To quantify this welfare loss, we assume that the willingness to pay of those who value the BBC at less than £5 tapers in a linear fashion from £5 to zero. On that basis we quantify the loss at £300 million. This is the difference between the total licence revenues paid by these viewers (£704 million) and the value to them of BBC programmes (£404 million). When account is taken of the welfare loss, the £2.77 billion contribution to national welfare of the licence-funded BBC can be decomposed into a consumer surplus of £3.07 billion enjoyed by those who believe that the BBC is worth at least the

---

7   *Measuring the Value of the BBC – A report by the BBC and Human Capital*, October 2004.

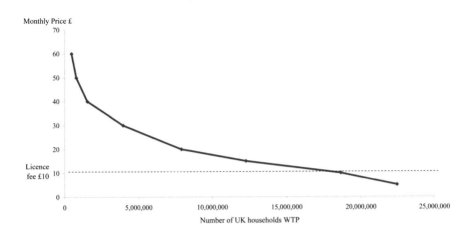

Figure 3. Demand curve for the BBC.

licence fee, and a consumer deficit (welfare loss) of £300 million suffered by those who do not think the BBC is worth the licence fee.

Subscription-funded BBC

Effect on revenues and programme spend

We assume that if the BBC were subscription funded, it would set the subscription at the revenue maximising level. Our estimate of the revenue maximising subscription, based on a logarithmic approximation to the demand curve, is £13.40 per month. This curve fitting approach makes maximum use of all the information extracted by the survey.[8] The resulting estimate is close to the figure of £13 per month in the BBC and Human Capital study.

At our estimated revenue-maximising price, 14.3 million households subscribe, generating £2.30 billion annually, £360 million less than current licence fee revenue. This shortfall may result in a reduction in quality of the BBC, which in turn affects the value consumers attach to the BBC. There is evidence that each £1 reduction of BBC's income could result in a fall in originated UK network programme spend by about 60p.[9] Applying this ratio implies a reduction in UK originated programme spending of £216 million in the subscription fee scenario – nearly 20 per cent of the current spending on UK-originated programmes.

---

8   We infer a best fit log-linear inverse demand curve.
9   Oliver & Ohlbaum, 2003.

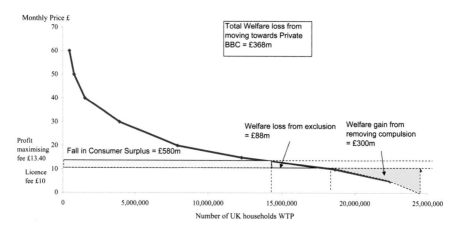

Figure 4. Demand curve for the BBC – maximising profit.

The reduction could be greater, if account is taken of the inevitable increase in the marketing budget needed to run the BBC as a subscription service. Such a reduction in programme budgets would clearly reduce the quality and range of PSB programming under a subscription scenario, which would in turn shift the demand curve for the BBC to the left, reducing revenue still further. There is no obvious end to this cycle of poorer programmes leading to smaller revenues, which is probably the major risk that would be incurred in turning the BBC into a subscription service.

Effect on welfare

In calculating the effect on welfare of a move to a voluntary subscription we have to consider three groups of viewers (see Figure 4):

- There are 14.3 million households who previously paid £10 per month and now pay £13.40 per month. The annual cost to this group of the move to a subscription-funded BBC is £580 million.

- There are 4.3 million viewers who were willing to pay £10 per month but less than £13. These viewers are better off by the amount of the licence fee, but worse off to the extent that they are now excluded from viewing programmes which they valued more highly than the licence fee. There is a net loss of £88 million,[10] shown by the smaller shaded triangle.

---

10 Welfare loss from exclusion = ½ x 4.3 x (13.40–10) = £7.3 million per month, or £87.6 million annually.

- Finally there are the 5.9 million viewers who were unwilling to pay £10 per month for the BBC, and who will certainly not pay £13.40 per month. These households save the licence fee, but lose the value of BBC programmes from which they are excluded. They are the only net gainers from the switch to voluntary subscription funding of the BBC and they gain £300 as explained above.

Table 6: Effect on welfare of a subscription funded BBC

	Willing to pay		
	More than £13.40 per month	**£10–13.40 per month**	**Less than £10 per month**
Number of viewers (million)	14.3	4.3	5.9
Change in licence fee per month	3.4	–10	–10
Total cost/saving per year (£m)	580	–519	–704
Value of programmes from which excluded per year (£m)	0	607	404
Net change in welfare (£m)	–580	–88	300

The results illustrated in Figure 4 and summarised in Table 6 are calculated by comparing a hypothetical voluntary subscription fee with the actual licence fee. To calculate the costs of compulsion, compared with the free-market benchmark of a subscription funded BBC, we can simply reverse the signs. This leads to the interesting conclusion that compulsion benefits those who place a high value on the BBC, who are generally the better off, at the expense of those who place a lower value. In this sense those who complain that the licence fee is a regressive tax are correct.

Tax-funded BBC

One way of overcoming this problem would be to move from licence fee funding to grant funding. Strictly speaking, since the marginal cost of supplying television programmes to additional viewers is zero, the socially optimal price for the BBC subscription is zero. At this price there would be no welfare loss from exclusion, and the entire value of the BBC would accrue to viewers in the form of consumer surplus.

This outcome could be achieved by funding the BBC with a grant, paid for out of general tax revenues. To ensure that the BBC delivered on its PSB remit, and generally satisfied the viewers, the grant would obviously be subject to regular review just like the licence fee. This option would ensure that the BBC was universally available on a free to air basis. There would be no welfare loss from exclusion. It would remove the worst feature of the present arrangement: a compulsory licence fee that is regarded by those who do not value the BBC as a (regressive) tax on television ownership.

However these gains come at a cost: the loss of £2.66 billion of revenue from the licence fee which would not be easily replaced. Although the licence fee is a flat-rate and therefore regressive tax, which is also expensive to collect, it is quite willingly paid. This is because everybody knows that the licence fee, unlike other taxes, does not help to fund defence spending or social security payments or any other form of public spending of which they might disapprove. The revenue from the tax is earmarked for a specific purpose, which is to pay for the BBC. As such it is viewed by most people as a reasonable charge for BBC services rather than a regressive tax on television sets.

Taxes whose revenue is allocated to a specific purpose are known as hypothecated taxes. The main advantage of hypothecation is that it increases willingness to pay. The original road fund licence, a tax on car ownership that survives to this day as Vehicle Excise Duty, was willingly paid because motorists were told that the money would be spent on roads. However, hypothecated taxes are not generally well regarded by public finance theorists because there is usually little connection between the revenues from such taxes and the spending requirements they are intended to meet. Total taxes on motorists today far outweigh spending on roads and we do not link tobacco taxes to the health service because the amount we spend on health should be decided by health needs, not by the revenue that happens to be generated by taxing smokers.

By comparison with these examples, however, the licence fee is much better suited to hypothecation. The tax rate can be (and is) regularly reviewed to ensure that tax revenues exactly match broadcasting needs. The revenues are not spent, and are known not to be spent, on any other purpose. For these reasons the licence fee is more like a charge than a tax. The licence payer knows what he is getting for his money. As a result the licence fee is probably more willingly paid than (for example) an equivalent increase in the income tax (0.75 pence). This is an important reason why licence fee funding is preferred to grant funding and will continue to be for the foreseeable future.

Conclusion

The argument of this essay can be briefly summarised as follows:

- Although broadcasting is now excludable, it remains non-rival; this means that most of the arguments from welfare economics for public provision of goods with a zero marginal cost remain intact. The fact that you now can charge for broadcasting does not mean that you should.

- Because the old arguments for PSB based on provision of programmes for niche audiences have weakened, the case must rest on the desirability of using public funds to encourage the production of quality television programmes which serve certain public purposes

- It has long been understood that advertising funded broadcasters have little incentive to make such programmes. In the past they have been obliged to by the terms of their commercial licences. However, the erosion in value of those licences makes the imposition of PSB obligations on commercial broadcasters much more difficult.

- There is no reason in principle why subscription-funded broadcasters should not make PSB programmes but an examination of the television market reveals that in practice they do not to any significant degree.

- This leaves the BBC as the most likely provider of PSB, but raises the question as to whether it could do so as a subscription service. This would have the advantage of ending the compulsory licence fee, which imposes welfare losses on those who do not value the output of the BBC.

- However, our analysis of the demand for BBC services, based on a willingness to pay survey conducted by the BBC and Human Capital, shows that the replacement of compulsory licence fee by voluntary subscriptions would increase the cost to viewers by 30 per cent, reduce revenues by 14 per cent and could reduce programme spend by as much as 20 per cent

- The welfare losses imposed by replacing the licence fee with (higher) voluntary subscription charges outweigh the gains. These losses could be avoided by a move to grant funding, but that would cost the public purse £2.66 billion in licence fee revenue. It would be hard to find another source for this tax revenue which would be so willingly paid.

References

Christian Koboldt, Sarah Hogg and Bill Robinson, 'The Implications of Funding for Broadcasting Output' in *Public Purposes in Broadcasting: Funding the BBC*, 1999.

Ofcom, *Review of Public Service Television Broadcasting, Phase 1: Is Television Special*, 2004.

Ofcom, *Review of Public Service Television Broadcasting, Phase 2: Meeting the digital challenge*, 2004.

Ofcom, *The Communications Market 2004 – Television*, 11 August 2004.

Measuring the Value of the BBC – A report by the BBC and Human Capital, October 2004.

Communications Act 2003, Part 3: Television and Radio Services, Chapter 4.

Robin Mason, *A Year Under Ofcom*, October 2004.

Professor Patrick Barwise, *Independent Review of the BBC's Digital Television Services*, 2004.

Mediatique Ltd, *A Consideration of Aspects of the Pay-TV Market in the UK in the Absence of Public Service Obligations*, August 2004.

Oliver & Ohlbaum Associates Ltd, *UK Television Content in the Digital Age*, 2003.

BBC Annual Report, 2003.

ITV plc Annual Report, 2003.

Channel 4 Annual Report, 2003.

BSkyB Annual Report, 2004.

Key Note Market Report 2003 – Digital TV, *Key Note*, May 2003.

7

The BBC and Public Value

Gavyn Davies[1]

Introduction

This essay asks what we can learn from economics to inform the debate on the renewal of the BBC's Charter in 2006, and in particular what economics can contribute to the basic question of why the BBC should exist at all. Many of the BBC's supporters will be resistant to approaching questions about its value from an economic standpoint, since they tend to prefer arguments couched in social or cultural terms. But there is much in the unappealing language of economics which can help justify the role of the BBC.

I am going to argue that economics is relevant to more than a calculation of the consumer value to the BBC.

Making an economic case for the BBC

There is a line of thought, widely held, that the core case for the BBC should rest not on money and markets, but on culture and citizenship. I agree. I have argued elsewhere[2] that the concept of public value should lie at the heart of the BBC's Charter bid. Some elements of public value – such as the price the consumer would pay to view a Premiership football match – can be readily measured in monetary terms in the marketplace. But other elements – such as the value

---

1   This essay is based on a lecture given by Gavyn Davies at the Said Business School, Oxford, on 10 June 2004, and it was first published in this form by the Social Market Foundation in December 2004.
2   A recent lecture at Hertford College, Oxford.

placed by society as a whole on an informed electorate – cannot be so easily valued, or even sensibly valued at all.

This has led some observers to argue that economics is only relevant to a part of what the BBC should be expected to provide, and that the consumer value of the BBC is the rightful subject matter of the economist. The citizen value, on the other hand, lies outside the purview of the economist. Ofcom, among many others, is prone to this type of assertion.

There is nothing intrinsically wrong with this distinction, especially as it makes clear that there are a number of facets to the Corporation's value. However, as a professional economist, I am slightly offended by it, since it entirely forgets that economics is not simply about what can be measured in market exchanges, but is also about all those things which cannot be so measured, but which need to be considered when designing policy. Much of the subject matter of economics concerns the problems that arise when markets are missing, or when important relationships between individuals are *not* captured by monetary exchanges.

These causes of market failure form the core justification for public intervention in private activity, and always have done, from Adam Smith onwards. It can be frustrating for economists to listen to confident opinions being expressed by commentators who appear blissfully oblivious to the fact that two centuries of detailed economic thought has already been devoted to precisely the matters under discussion. It would be perverse to ignore these economic principles during the Charter debate.

In order to justify the existence of the BBC in its present form, there are at least three large questions which need to be addressed. These are:

1. Are there market failures in the private broadcasting market which imply that the market does not function efficiently, and therefore justify government intervention?

2. Are there distributional failings in the free market system, implying that the market (though possibly efficient) is unable to allocate information and entertainment satisfactorily to all citizens?

3. If public intervention in the market is justified on either of these grounds, are there alternative forms of intervention or regulation which would be preferable to the BBC?

I focus primarily on the first of these questions, since this is where the most serious intellectual attacks on the BBC are now to be found. It is incontrovertible that a necessary condition for the BBC to exist is that there is a market failure in the private broadcasting market in the UK. Otherwise, why would we want to go to all the trouble of collecting a licence fee, and using it to create a massive public body like the BBC? It would be much simpler just to leave all this to the private sector, if we believed that the free market produces an optimal out-turn.

A market failure in Reithian television services

It used to be widely accepted that there was a clear market failure in broadcasting. There was a severe shortage of spectrum, leading to a restricted choice of channels, and there was no way of charging people directly for channels or programmes individually. But now there is virtually no shortage of spectrum, and many homes have access to the encryption technology which implies that channels can be bought and sold like any other free market service. This has led many to conclude that the television market is now just like any other, and that the case for market failure has therefore dropped away.

It is my view that free markets are generally, indeed almost always, the first and best default option for the organisation of human activity. But that does not mean that they are always and everywhere optimal. Sometimes markets can fail. Is this the case in the broadcasting market? More precisely, is this the case for the service which BBC television seeks to provide? This needs to be seen as a package of channels, which are together intended to inform, educate and entertain the viewer. The BBC package is explicitly intended to reach the mass market, not the tiny niche which is reached by PBS in America. I shall call this the market for Reithian services.

It is important to be clear what we mean by a market failure in the area of Reithian broadcasting. Market failure exists when there is an under-provision of Reithian broadcasting services under free market conditions, relative to the socially optimum level. As in any other field of micro-economics, the socially optimum level occurs when the marginal social benefit is exactly equal to the marginal social cost. If the marginal benefit is greater than the marginal cost, then more Reithian services should be produced, and vice versa.

Many of my former colleagues at the BBC were extremely reluctant to hinge any argument for the BBC's existence on the concept of market failure. Since this concept is so widely misunderstood and misrepresented, I could readily understand their reluctance in doing so. But as a rigorous economist, their reluctance made no sense at all. Without market failure, the government should not intervene in the commercial market-place, and the BBC should be privatised.

The confusion about this arises, I believe, because people misunderstand what economists mean by market failure. The term is frequently over-interpreted. So it is vital to say explicitly what I do *not* mean when I use this particular term of art.

First, I do not mean that Reithian broadcasting will be entirely absent from a free market system. If the BBC did not exist, there would still be a great deal of Reithian television produced by ITV, Channel 4, the excellent Sky News and other commercial providers. But there may not be enough to attain the social optimum level.

Second, I do not mean that the BBC should produce only those programmes which are absent in the market place, while focusing solely on unique, minority content. Since practically everything is produced to some degree by the free market, such a rule would soon leave the BBC producing absolutely nothing at all.

I therefore reject the fear that the market failure case automatically implies that the BBC will become an increasingly irrelevant provider of up-market niche channels. What it does imply is that the BBC should top-up the supply of mass market Reithian broadcasting which comes from the private sector.

Causes of market failure in Reithian broadcasting

The subject of welfare economics has established that a free market will result in a socially optimal level of production of any good or service under certain conditions. These conditions include perfect competition, the absence of externalities, decreasing returns to scale, no missing markets, and no asymmetries of information. If these and a few other conditions hold, we would expect the free operation of supply and demand to result in an optimal or 'efficient' level of output. Economists call this a Pareto-optimal situation, and it implies that no-one in the economy can be made better off without making someone else worse off. It represents the beautiful result of the free working of the price mechanism. For most goods and services, governments should get out of the way and watch the price mechanism do its magical work.

However, this is not always the case. Figure 1 shows a stylized version of how deviations from the assumptions of welfare economics might affect the market for Reithian services. In the diagram, the private demand and supply curves intersect at Qp, which is the amount of Reithian television which would be produced in a pure commercial market. However, let us now assume that some of the benefits of such television are not paid for directly by consumers, but are valued only by society as a whole. Such benefits might be the average level of

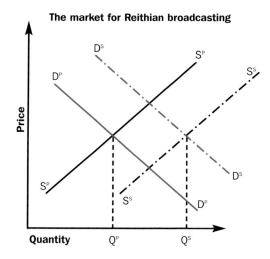

The market for Reithian broadcasting

Dp and Sp are the private demand and supply curves.

Ds and Ss are the social demand and supply curves, allowing for positive consumption and production externalities.

Since Qs>Qp, there is a market failure in the production of Reithian broadcasting.

Figure 1. Difference between free market and socially optimum level of output.

information possessed by all citizens, or the general availability of cultural programmes.

If these items are generally valued, but not directly purchased by individual subscribers to TV channels, then the social demand curve for Reithian television will be to the right of the private demand curve, and the optimal quantity Qs will exceed the amount produced in a free market. In such circumstances, the role of the BBC is to fill the gap between the amount of Reithian services that would be produced by the commercial sector, and the higher quantity which is implied by the social optimum.

There are in fact four main reasons why there is market failure in the UK broadcasting market. These represent clear deviations from the assumptions which are required in welfare economics to ensure that the free market produces a socially optimum result. The reasons are:

1. Broadcasting remains a public good, which implies that it should be provided without making a charge at the point of use.

2. Broadcasting involves the creation of inter-personal relationships, called externalities, which are not fully reflected in market transactions.

3. Broadcasting involves increasing returns to scale, which tends to lead to the existence of private monopolies in a free market.

4.   Broadcasting involves informational deficiencies which lead to sub-optimal levels of demand for quality products from consumers in the free market.

None of these assertions is remotely new. They have been widely discussed in the literature, including in previous work by myself and Andrew Graham,[3] and also in my government report on BBC funding in 1999.[4] They, together with a departure from the list of the assumptions required for Pareto optimality listed earlier, effectively capture the causes of market failure. Sometimes, an eager new author will come up with a fresh twist on these old favourites (such as the invention of the importance of citizenship, which is simply a particular type of externality), but the novelty usually turns out to be more apparent than real.

Broadcasting: a public good in the digital age

It is important to revisit these causes of market failure because they have not disappeared simply because technology has gone digital, despite assumptions to the contrary. Indeed, they will be with us for a very long time.

The first issue for consideration is whether broadcasting is still a public good. Public goods or services have two characteristics. The first is that they are non-rivalrous, which means that consumption of the service by one individual does not preclude consumption of that same good by another individual. Street lighting is an obvious example. This implies that the marginal cost of supplying the good to successive individuals is effectively zero, once the original costs of production have been incurred. Furthermore, it implies that the price charged for the service should also be zero, since any positive charge will prevent some consumers from enjoying a product which could be supplied to them for nothing. I do not see how this can be described as optimal by anyone who has studied welfare economics.

The second characteristic of public goods is that they are non-excludable, which means that consumption by one individual makes it impossible to exclude any other individual from having the opportunity to consume the same benefits. National defence is a prime example. The implication of non-excludability is that it is impossible to make a charge for the product, since no-one will choose to pay for a product that is freely available to all. Therefore no private market

3   Graham, A. and Davies, G. (1997) *Broadcasting, Society and Policy in the Multimedia Age*. University of Luton Press.
4   Davies, G. *et al.* (1999) *The Future Funding of the BBC: Report of the Independent Review Panel*. London: Department of Culture, Media and Sport.

will develop for the product, and it has to be provided through the public sector.

Traditional analogue broadcasting fulfils both of these requirements completely. Once the analogue signal has been provided for a single user, there is no extra cost for providing it to everyone in the same locality, so the product is clearly non-rivalrous. Furthermore, once you have provided the signal for any household, you cannot exclude all other households, so it is also non-excludable. It is in fact almost the perfect textbook example of a public good. To the extent that analogue broadcasting still exists (and by far the majority of television sets in the UK are able to receive only analogue signals), then television remains an archetypal public good.

However, this is not so obviously true of digital broadcasting, which is presumably one reason why some commentators believe that the arrival of digital services undermines the case for treating broadcasting as a public good. Digital broadcasting can be made excludable, via encryption of the signal along with set-top boxes inside each home. This means that a free market in television services can develop, since people can be charged for their use of individual channels and may be even individual programmes. However, this will not become feasible until analogue switchover, and even then most TV sets may not be equipped with the necessary boxes, since many Freeview boxes are being sold without a charging facility.

More importantly, digital broadcasting will still be non-rivalrous, just like its analogue predecessor. This will never change. The marginal cost of providing a satellite digital signal to all homes is effectively zero, once the satellite has been launched. So broadcasting will remain forever a public good, in the sense that the marginal cost of provision to additional users is negligible. This is a sufficient condition to suggest that a charge at the point of use would be inefficient, for the reasons explained above.

Figure 2 compares broadcasting with other public services, based on the extent to which the relevant services exhibit the characteristics of non-rivalry and non-excludability. The further upwards and to the right you move in the chart, the greater the extent that the requirements of a public good are met. Analogue broadcasting is almost a pure public good, alongside national defence and street lighting. Encrypted digital broadcasting is at the top left, with the likely state of the actual broadcasting market in 2015 somewhere around the middle top. This would still leave broadcasting at the end of the next Charter period exhibiting far more of the characteristics of a public good than many other services provided by the public sector – including health, education, vaccinations, the

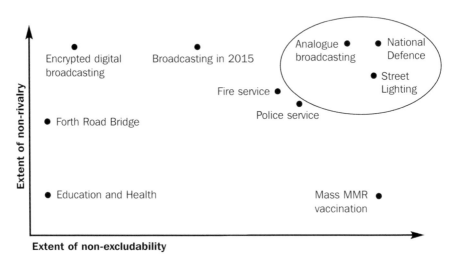

Figure 2. Broadcasting compared with other public goods.

Forth Road Bridge, and the fire and police services. Based on this graph, it is not clear why so many commentators wish to shift the BBC outside the public sector, while leaving these other services firmly inside it.

In summary, then, broadcasting will always remain non-rivalrous, so the optimal subscription charge at the point of use should be zero. Any attempt to exclude some users by levying a subscription may result in under-consumption and could be sub-optimal. And the technology required to put such a charging mechanism in place would be a waste of resources.

Some economists have argued that, just because a product is a public good, it does not automatically have to be produced in the state sector, and provided to the population at a user charge of zero. For example, David Lipsey has pointed out that the money to provide the service has to be raised through taxation, and that this might have disincentive effects elsewhere in the economy.[5] This is true in principle, but the BBC licence fee is in effect a lump sum charge on every household in the country, so the marginal disincentive effects are likely to be zero. (There will still be adverse effects on income distribution, which I will address later.)

Another argument, used by Martin Cave in his writings for Ofcom, is that many other goods and services, which are currently provided in the private sector, are

---

5   Commentary by David Lipsey in Gavyn Davies, *The BBC and Public Value*. SMF, December 2004.

How do we know what is the output level of a public good?

Derive a 'market demand curve' or social marginal benefit curve by vertically adding individual demand curves, shown alongside as D^A and D^B

Optimal output occurs where the resulting curve intersects the social marginal cost, or 'market supply curve', shown alongside as S

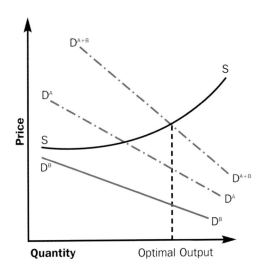

Figure 3. The optimal output of a public good.

characterised by zero marginal costs of production or distribution, so why should television be any different?[6] He claims that the market for television could be in the private sector without breaching Pareto optimality because some television programmes can be financed through advertising (with a zero user cost), while others could be sold into a differentiated market, charging each user precisely the amount they were willing to pay for the product. One example of this is to charge a high price for first run movies, and a much lower price for second and subsequent runs. If this could be done perfectly, it would not necessarily result in an under-provision of the 'public' good compared to the optimal output. However, there are other severe disadvantages attached to advertising funding; and I am very sceptical whether perfect price differentiation can ever be achieved for television services. In any event, Martin Cave says that a free market for British television would end up looking rather like the television landscape in the United States, which is precisely what some of us are trying to avoid!

If we accept that broadcasting remains a public good, how much of it should be produced in the UK? Figure 3 shows that the demand curve for a public good is derived by adding vertically the individual demand curves for every member of society. Obviously this is impossible in practice, but it is possible to derive a national demand curve for BBC services by asking samples of the population

---

6   Cave, M. (2004) *Competition in broadcasting – consequences for viewers.* Research Paper prepared for Ofcom.

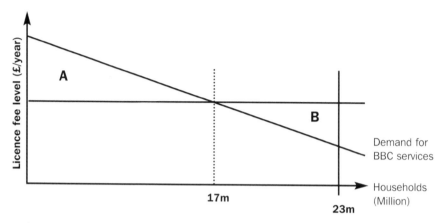

On rough estimates, about 17m households value BBC services at more than the current licence fee. These are gainers from the existence of the BBC.

About 6 million value the BBC at less than the current licence fee. These are the losers.

The net consumer surplus created is A minus B, estimated to be well over £2bn/year, or ¼% of GDP.

Figure 4. Consumer surplus created by the BBC. [Source: BBC Pilot Study, January 2004.]

how much they would be willing to pay for the entire package of BBC services, if they were available on subscription. Just before I left the BBC in January 2004, we were in the process of doing this, with the research being carried out by Human Capital.[7] Figure 4 shows the results of a preliminary study, which was a pilot, but the data does not seem to have changed much since then (see Chapter 4).

About 17 million households, or more than three-quarters of the population in the UK, value the BBC at or above the £121 per year which they are charged in the licence fee. About one third of the population would be willing to pay double the licence fee, and more than one quarter would be willing to pay treble the licence fee. Thus the vast majority of the population are gainers from the existence of the BBC, with many gaining by a very large amount.

However, around 6 million households say that they value the BBC at less than the current licence fee. Whether they would in practice refuse to pay £121 per year if they actually tried to live without the BBC is not clear, but that is certainly what they say today. Of these 6 million, it is quite likely that a large number

---

7   Human Capital (2004) Research on projecting take-up for digital services prepared for the BBC.

actually refuse to pay the licence fee, and are not caught in any given year. This might lower the total by about 1.5 million, leaving about 4.5 million households who actually pay the licence fee while attaching a lower value to the BBC's services than the cost of the licence fee. These are the losers from the current compulsory system of funding the BBC, though most of them do not lose by very much, since even they generally assign a positive value to BBC services.

It is right for the BBC to worry about these people, and to tailor some of their services towards addressing the problem. It does not seem to me impossible to eliminate this problem entirely by shifting BBC priorities somewhat towards those who are currently underserved, many of whom will probably be in the ethnic minorities, will be on lower incomes, and will be located outside the south east of England. Former BBC Director General Greg Dyke was very aware of this problem, and was addressing it very effectively. However, more needs to be done during the new Charter, and I expect Mark Thompson to be alive to the task. A disaffected minority is dangerous for the BBC and for the licence fee system. It has never been a feature of the BBC in the past, and it should remain a priority to eliminate the problem in the future.

The problem, however, must be seen in context. Those who gain from the existence of the BBC vastly outweigh those who lose, both in raw numbers and in monetary terms. By my estimation, the amount gained exceeds the amount lost by well over £2 billion a year, equivalent to 0.25 per cent of GDP. This amount of consumer surplus would be instantly lost if the BBC were closed down.

This may be what explains the extraordinary and enduring popularity of the BBC as a public service in the UK. These figures also provide a strong, long-term economic case for the BBC.

The impact of privatisation on the BBC

Those who deny that broadcasting is a public good usually argue that channels and programmes should be financed in the market just like any other service. In the old days, the recommended method for privately financing the BBC was usually advertising revenue, but since the Peacock Report in the late 1980s, the fatal flaws in this option have been widely recognised. Instead, those who believe in privatising the BBC's revenue stream usually recommend that the BBC should become a subscription service. If this were to happen, the BBC might choose to charge a licence fee which maximised its overall revenue (Figure 5).

I estimate that this might be around £170 per year, at which point about 13 million households would choose to pay the new charge, and about 10 million

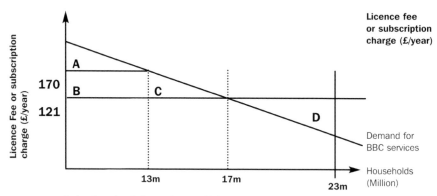

Under the subscription model, the BBC would probably charge a revenue maximising subscription charge of (say) £170/year

About 6 million consumers would benefit, by an amount equivalent to D.
The rest would lose an amount equivalent to C+B.

Assuming B+C>D, the total amount of consumer surplus would fall under a subscription model compared to the licence fee system

Figure 5. The impact of a subscription model on consumer surplus.
[Source: BBC Pilot Study, January 2004.]

would choose to lose the services of the BBC. Clearly, the ability of the BBC to provide universal services for the whole nation would be lost overnight – a sacrifice which I for one would not be prepared to make.

Some people would, however, probably welcome such a shift in policy. These would be the 6 million households who currently value the BBC at less than the licence fee. Everyone else would lose part of their consumer surplus if there were a shift to a subscription system. About four million would lose all of their consumer surplus because they would no longer subscribe to the BBC at all, while about 13 million would subscribe, but would see their consumer surplus declining because they would now be paying about £170 per year for the BBC instead of the current £121 per year.

Overall, there would be a large drop of about £0.5 billion in national welfare if the BBC shifted from a licence fee system to a subscription system. This could only be justified if one placed a very high weight indeed on the welfare of those 6 million households who would welcome such a change, and placed rather a low weight on the welfare of everyone else. Rather than conducting intellectual distortions to do this, I would prefer to eliminate the problem of the 6 million by addressing the underserved directly, as discussed earlier.

So the existence of the BBC adds enormously to the total welfare of the country, compared either to a situation in which the BBC were closed down, or to a situation in which the BBC were privatised and allowed to behave like any other commercial company, financing itself through subscription revenues. Many people dislike the licence fee system on political grounds, and many others seem to have persuaded themselves that changes in technology should lead inexorably to the BBC becoming a subscription based service. These people should face up directly to the large welfare losses which would immediately be incurred if their ideas came to fruition. They need to address the question of how the nation would be compensated for these losses.

The optimal scale of the BBC

If we accept that the BBC continues to produce a public good which adds to national welfare, this still leaves an important question about the optimum scale of the BBC itself. One way of looking at this is to define the core television service of the BBC to be BBC One, and then ask whether the marginal benefit derived from extra services exceeds the marginal cost of providing them. If so, then perhaps the BBC is too big. It is easy to measure the marginal costs of extra television services, and these are shown on a per household and per head basis in Figure 6.

Essentially, it is worth providing BBC Two if the average individual is willing to value the service at just under £7 *per year* – not per week or per month. The values that need to be placed on BBC Three, BBC Four and News 24 are on average less than £1 per year for each citizen. I would make the confident assertion that an average individual would place at least that amount of value on these services, noting that the cheapest Sky package, excluding sport, costs about £150 per annum. If this is indeed the case, then I would argue that the recent expansion of BBC television into the digital world has already added further to national welfare.

Other causes of market failure

Even if the public good arguments for the BBC are not accepted, there are several important other sources of market failure in the market for Reithian broadcasting. Ofcom seem to want to lump these together as 'citizenship' arguments, but I see them as being grounded firmly in welfare economics.

To start with, many types of externalities clearly exist in broadcasting. These are linkages between the welfare of individuals which are never traded in exchange for money. If an individual feels better off because other people are better informed or educated, this effect will never be captured in free market prices,

	Per Household (£ per year)	Per Head (£ per year)
BBC2	15.58	6.67
BBC3	3.39	1.45
BBC4	1.75	0.75
News24	1.78	0.76

For comparison, the cheapest Sky package (no sport) costs £150 per annum, while the full package costs £582 per annum.

Figure 6. Does marginal benefit for willingness to pay exceed the following marginal costs?

and programmes which contribute to information and education will be under-provided in a commercial system. These effects are well known, as are the negative externalities which are triggered when some citizens choose to access pornographic or violent programming. Less familiar are the externalities which are created when television is the catalyst for communities of interest to develop.

These allow individuals to derive greater enjoyment from their enthusiasms because they are shared with many other people. As Martin Brookes has recently pointed out in an important paper, these externalities apply just as much to football and Eastenders as they do to opera and politics.[8] They offer a clear economic justification for the BBC to be involved in popular programming.

A further form of market failure stems from the fact that broadcasting tends to be an industry in which there are high fixed costs (for example, the cost of launching a satellite), and much lower variable costs. There are therefore substantial economies of scale and scope which result in marginal costs declining as the scale of the firm increases. The minimum efficient scale of a broadcaster will tend to be large, leading to a lack of competition and eventually to monopoly. Monopoly producers will over-charge for their products, and the quantity produced will be much less than the social optimum.

Those who think this is all rather far-fetched should consider the recent history

8   Brookes, M. (2004) *Watching Alone: Social Capital and Public Service Broadcasting.* The Work Foundation in partnership with the BBC.

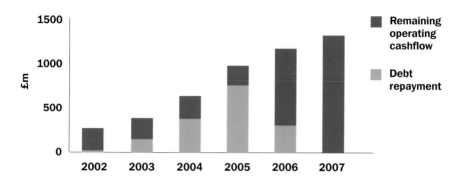

Figure 7. Sky operating cashflow and debt. [Source: Goldman Sachs.]

of the television market in the UK. BSkyB, after knocking out BSB, grew its revenue from nothing to £3 billion in just over a decade. It is now larger than the BBC. ITV has struggled against this competition, and forces to consolidate ITV further, and then sell to a foreign buyer, are strong. According to some forecasts, Sky's free cash flow will rise several fold in the next few years, reaching well over £1 billion in 2007.

Sky is becoming a colossus compared to ITV, which now exhibits a business model which is clearly under threat (Figure 8). It would be surprising if ITV's advertising revenue rose at all during the current decade, since ITV's audience share has fallen by about one third over ten years. The only way in which ITV has been able to stabilise its revenue in the face of these plummeting audiences has been to increase its advertising rates substantially. But it is increasingly questionable whether advertisers will be willing to pay premium rates for access to a declining minority audience. This squeeze may pose an ever-greater threat to the ability of ITV to afford the kind of public service programming which it has been able to make in the past. Ofcom will no doubt fight strongly against these trends, but I have only limited faith in the power of outside regulators to hold back the powerful forces of the market.

In my opinion, these trends will increase the importance of the BBC as a provider of mass public service broadcasting, and as a bulwark against the possible future dominance of Sky. But even the BBC will find this a hard task (Figure 9). Many observers have suggested that the BBC has been over-funded in recent years, and it is true that its revenue has grown relative to ITV. But the growth of Sky has out-stripped everyone, including the BBC. While this is an eloquent testimony to the strength of Sky's consumer offering (and I yield to no-one in my admiration for Sky as a commercial endeavour), UK needs to ask itself

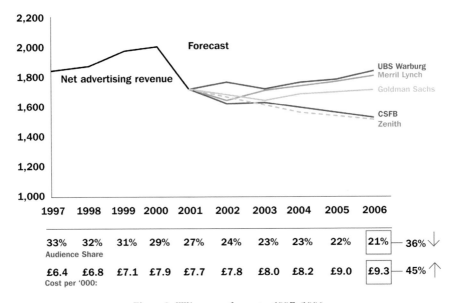

Figure 8. ITV revenue forecasts, 1997–2006.
[Sources: Zenith Media; CSFB; Merril Lynch, Goldman Sachs; UBS Warburg; BBC Corporate Strategy.]

whether it wants Sky to be so much bigger than anyone else, including the BBC, in a few years time.

Far from expanding relative to its competition, the BBC's share of broadcasting revenue has continued to shrink in the past decade (Figure 10). And if the licence fee rises only in line with the Retail Price Index (RPI) in the next Charter period, this relative decline in the size of the BBC will accelerate. Its share of industry revenue will fall to under 20 per cent by 2015, leaving it struggling to play its traditional role as the standard setter in British broadcasting.

The trend in the broadcasting market is towards fewer, bigger players, with Sky in particular being likely to exert increasing market power. Market failure on this score is increasing, not diminishing. And the BBC is shrinking in its relative size, making it harder for it to redress this market failure. Yet, in the face of all this evidence, the BBC's competitors and some politicians routinely castigate the BBC for being of frightening scale.

I doubt if the BBC itself will have the temerity to fly in the face of this misguided tide of opinion by asking the government for a licence fee settlement in excess of inflation, for fear of being laughed out of court. But the truth is that no other public service in UK – not the health service, not the schools, not the army and

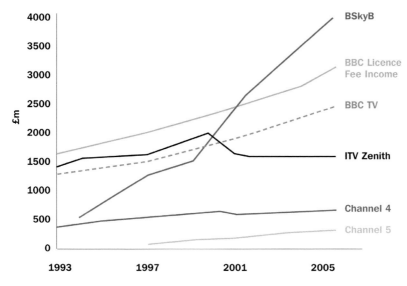

Figure 9. BBC income vs. its competitors.

definitely not the police – would ever contemplate accepting a decade-long settlement in which its income is frozen in real terms. Such a miserly outcome should not be seen as a 'good' settlement for the BBC, our consistently most successful public service throughout its eighty-year life.

The last source of market failure is informational deficiency. This is extremely

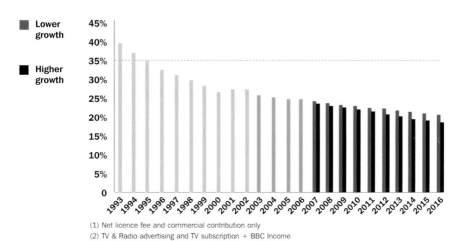

(1) Net licence fee and commercial contribution only
(2) TV & Radio advertising and TV subscription + BBC Income

Figure 10. BBC income[1] as a percentage of industry revenue[2].
[Source: Zenith, UBS Warburg, BBC Financial & Commercial Strategy.]

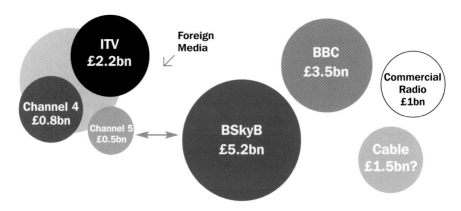

Figure 11. UK broadcasters' revenues, 2010 forecast.
[Source: Goldman Sachs, Merrill Lynch, CSFB, UBS Warburg, BBC Corporate Finance.]

familiar territory. Some goods and services need to be experienced by consumers before they can be fully appreciated. Education is normally thought to be such an 'experience' good. Free market provision results in under-consumption, and therefore too little formation of human capital. This is close to the case for Reithian television, a complex set of services the benefits of which become clear only after considerable sampling and experience. The free market will not encourage such experience, which needs to be nurtured through marketing, scheduling and programme making skills. And this is hard to achieve through the attentions of a regulator like Ofcom, since it is so hard to define precisely in a contract. Hence the need for an institution like the BBC, which does all of this because it is built into its DNA.

So it seems to me clear that there are many sources of market failure for the BBC to address, and it is also clear that different genres have different degrees of market failure attached to them (Figure 12).

Few market failures are apparent, you will be pleased to hear, in the fields of pornographic or violent conduct, and rather few in the area of imported mass entertainment. It would not be the end of the world if the BBC were absent from these genres. On the other hand, mainstream popular entertainment, produced at home, does exhibit several key elements of market failure, and there are therefore good reasons for a strong BBC presence in this genre. And of course, the most serious market failures are in the fields of news, information and education, so this is where the BBC's presence should be most pronounced. Given this pecking order of market failure, it is of considerable comfort that countless surveys of audience opinion show that the public believes that the

Type of television service	Public good		Externalities create 'Public Value' or 'Social Capital?'	Economics of scale in production?*	Information asymmetrics?
	Non-rival?	Non-excludable?			
Pornographic/ violent content	Yes	No – always encrypted	Strongly negative	Yes	No
Imported mass entertainment	Yes	Often encrypted	Mildly positive	Yes	Unlikely
Mainstream popular entertainment	Yes	Yes	Positive	Strongly positive	Possible
Informative/ educative content	Yes	Yes	Strongly positive	Strongly positive	Strong

Potentially leading to monopoly at high concentration

Figure 12. Summary of market failures in television and radio.

BBC's strengths relative to its competition correspond precisely to what this theory says is appropriate.

Distributional failures

This is also reassuring from the point of view of so-called distributional failures (Figure 13).

These are not strictly in the same camp as the market inefficiencies which we have just been discussing, but they are nevertheless important further reasons for public intervention in commercial activity. If society is dissatisfied with the distributional consequences of the free market, it can legitimately decide to redistribute income and wealth, even though the required policies (taxation and public expenditure) may result in a breach of overall economic efficiency. A fairer distribution of resources, even in a less efficient economy, can sometimes be deemed to be a better overall outcome for society.

If redistribution is deemed desirable, this can be done via direct provision of specific goods and services. For example, most societies opt for a minimum compulsory provision of education services. This direct provision usually occurs when goods are deemed to be so-called 'merit goods'. These goods are believed

Type of television service	Distributional concerns?
Pornographic/violent content	No
Mainstream popular entertainment	No
Informative/educative content	yes – this is a 'merit good' implying concerns about under-provision to low income groups

This table shows concerns about whether the service will be provided in acceptable quantities to all income groups under a free market

Figure 13. Distribution concerns about provision.

to be desirable in themselves, even if this overrides market preferences. Reithian broadcasting, which promotes learning, the growth of human capital and good citizenship, can be argued to be a merit good which should be subject to a minimum national provision. Once again, distributional concerns are much more powerful in the traditional BBC genres than they are in genres usually more associated with the commercial sector.

Conclusions

1. Market failure is a necessary condition for the BBC to exist in its present form. It is not a sufficient condition, but those who hope to justify the existence of the BBC without placing market failure at the centre of their case are facing an uphill intellectual struggle.

2. Despite widespread assertions that market failure in the broadcasting market is being eliminated by technical change, the free market in the new Charter period would continue to result in an under-provision of Reithian broadcasting services, relative to the social optimum. Broadcasting will remain a public good in the digital world.

3. The BBC is one way of addressing this persistent market failure, thus ensuring that an under-provision of Reithian broadcasting does not occur.

Public sector activity	Public good		Positive externalities	Increasing returns	Information asymmetries	Distributional concerns
	Non-rival	Non-excludable				
Health	No	No	Yes	No	Yes	Yes
Education	No	No	Yes	No	Yes	Yes
Defence	Yes	Yes	No	Yes	Yes	No
Law & Order	Partly	Partly	Yes	No	No	No
Roads	Partly	No	Slight	No	No	No
Reithian Broadcasting	Yes	Yes	Yes	Yes	Yes	Yes

Figure 14. Market and distribution failures in the UK public sector.

It is not the only way, but it is the way that the UK has chosen, and it is probably the best way.

4. The BBC, funded by a licence fee of over £120 per year, creates well over £2 billion of consumer surplus, or national welfare, each year. In order to maintain its ability to contribute this amount to national welfare, the BBC should not be allowed to shrink in relative terms. This is exactly what would happen, notably relative to Sky, with a real terms freeze for the licence fee in the new Charter.

5. A subscription-based BBC would exclude 10 million households from receiving the BBC, and would generate much less consumer welfare than the current licence fee system. There would be some net gainers from a switch to subscription, but they would be in a minority, and the nation as a whole would lose. Nevertheless, the needs of the minority – probably concentrated among the ethnic minorities, the lower income groups, and those outside the south east of England – are important and should be addressed by re-orienting parts of the BBC's output to take account of their particular requirements. This does not imply dumbing down.

6. While the BBC is not the only way of addressing market failure, alternative models for government intervention and regulation are at best unproven. Ofcom will be severely stretched to prevent the commercial sector from moving towards greater monopoly along with less public service

broadcasting. It should focus its attention on this massive task, rather than seeking to extend its power over the BBC.

7. Market failure is in some ways much more obvious in broadcasting than it is in health and education, which are not public goods (Figure 14). Other public services like law and order and the road system also exhibit fewer of the characteristics of market failure than Reithian broadcasting. People should remember this before calling on the BBC to be privatised.

8. Those who argue that changes in technology have eliminated the case for the BBC are wrong.

References

Brookes, M. (2004) *Watching Alone: Social Capital and Public Service Broadcasting*. The Work Foundation in partnership with the BBC.

Cave, M. (2004) *Competition in broadcasting – consequences for viewers*. Research Paper prepared for Ofcom.

Davies, G. *et al* (1999) *The Future Funding of the BBC: Report of the Independent Review Panel*. London: Department of Culture, Media and Sport.

Graham, A. and Davies, G. (1997) *Broadcasting, Society and Policy in the Multimedia Age*. University of Luton Press.

8

Contestable Funding: Lessons from New Zealand

Jeremy Mayhew and Luke Bradley-Jones

1. Introduction[1]

Funding for public service broadcasting (PSB) is a key element of any broadcasting regulatory framework: the scale, source, and means of allocation of public funding can directly affect the form and effectiveness of PSB delivery. The PSB funding arrangements in the UK are currently being reviewed by the Government, as part of the BBC's Charter Review, and by Ofcom, in its first quinquennial PSB Review.

One possible approach to PSB funding is a contestable funding model, whereby public money is allocated from a central fund to broadcasters (or direct to producers), via a competitive tendering process, to support specified production activities (e.g. of a programme or series). This type of model has been in place in New Zealand since 1989 and continues to be the primary means of funding PSB delivery today. This essay sets out to assess how, in practice, the model works – and how effectively it has served its intended purposes and wider PSB goals.[2]

---

1   We would like to acknowledge Paul Norris's essay, 'Reshaping Public Broadcasting, the New Zealand Experience 1988–2003' as a source of interesting and relevant information and analysis of PSB in New Zealand. This essay can be found in the ippr publication *Public Service Communications*, January 2004.

2   This essay only considers public service *television* broadcasting; indeed the contestable funding model in New Zealand is only used for television funding, even though public funding is provided for public radio and a range of other services.

This essay is structured as follows:

- Section 2 provides a summary of the evolution of the PSB sector in New Zealand over the past twenty years

- Section 3 describes, in greater detail, how New Zealand's contestable funding system works

- Section 4 assesses the strengths and limitations of the New Zealand model

- Section 5 considers whether any lessons can be drawn for the UK debate from the New Zealand experience.

One theme in particular runs throughout our analysis: what are the advantages and disadvantages of a contract-based approach, such as contestable funding, to PSB provision? We address this question in our assessment of the New Zealand model and, in the final section, ask whether any advantages of such an approach could be combined with those of a PSB system which is based around strong PSB institutions.

In the context of the current UK public policy debate, New Zealand's PSB funding model makes for interesting analysis: some aspects have worked well, others not so well. It is worth bearing in mind, however, that the New Zealand market is fundamentally different from the UK's, in two main respects. First, the PSB and wider broadcasting sector is much smaller than the UK's, in every respect. Second, as will become evident in the next section, over the past twenty years, New Zealand PSB has operated and evolved within a highly political environment, with successive governments bringing radical, and radically different, agendas to the broadcasting sector. This changing environment has had as much of an effect on the evolution of the sector as any other factor, including the contestable funding system.

2. A brief history of PSB in New Zealand

Before considering in greater detail the arrangements and the merits of the New Zealand contestable funding model, it is worth briefly setting out the historical context for these arrangements and the evolution of the PSB model over the past twenty years to its current state.

An overview of New Zealand's broadcasting market

New Zealand is a small country, with a population of 4 million people and an annual GDP per capita in 2003 of around NZ$27,000 (equivalent to around UK£11,000, compared to UK£17,000 in the UK).[3] The population is made up

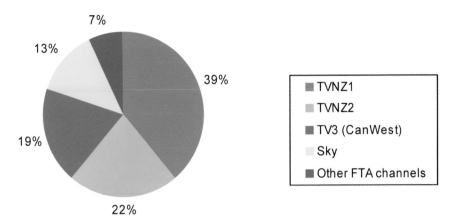

Figure 1. 2003 audience share, by broadcaster (%). [Source: TVNZ Screen Digest.]

of a number of different ethnic groups, with indigenous Maoris accounting for around 15 per cent of the population, Asian migrants 7 per cent, and Pacific Islanders also 7 per cent.

The New Zealand broadcasting industry is made up of a mix of free-to-air and pay-TV broadcasters. The main terrestrial broadcasters, accounting for over 95 per cent of the market, are TV New Zealand (TVNZ), the state-owned incumbent, which has 2 main channels (TV1 and TV2), and CanWest, the Canadian media group, which operates TV3 and C4. The satellite operator Sky, owned by News Corp, is the only pay-TV operator in the country.

TVNZ remains the dominant player, with 61 per cent audience share across its 2 main channels in 2003, followed by TV3 with 19 per cent. Sky's share across all of New Zealand's 1.4 million homes is 13 per cent; other channels account for 7 per cent.

Pay-TV penetration in New Zealand is approximately 42 per cent, while digital penetration stands at 32 per cent – all of which is accounted for by Sky's digital subscribers (DTT has not yet been launched and there is no cable operator).

Advertising revenues remain the dominant source of income for New Zealand's broadcasting market. In 2003, out of total revenues for the sector of approximately NZ$1 billion (£UK397 million), TV advertising spend accounted for NZ$592 million (UK£224 million),[4] while pay-TV subscription revenues

---

3   Source: Economist Intelligence Unit.

4   Assuming exchange rate of NZ$2.64 to the UK£.

were NZ$331 million (£125 million), and public funding (direct and indirect) for TV broadcasting reached NZ$125 million (UK£47 million).[5]

Evolution of the PSB sector

As the publicly owned public service broadcaster, TVNZ has been and remains the dominant PSB provider in New Zealand. Since the mid-1980s, however, both the level of PSB delivery and the means of delivery have evolved significantly.

Under the 1976 Broadcasting Act, TVNZ, as part of the then 'Broadcasting Corporation of New Zealand' (BCNZ), was a 'Crown-owned Company' (CROC) with a remit to serve explicit public purposes, including the reflection and fostering of national culture and identity. BCNZ ran radio and TV services and was funded by a combination of a universal licence fee and advertising revenues. This mixed funding arrangement had been in place since the organisation's inception in 1961, justified on the grounds that the licence fee alone would not generate sufficient revenues to support a range of broadcasting services, given the relatively small population of New Zealand.

During the course of the 1980s, BCNZ became increasingly commercially orientated, for two main reasons. First, as TV penetration and usage increased, the scope for growth in advertising revenues was significant. By the mid-1980s, 85 per cent of the broadcaster's revenues were commercial. Second, the Labour Government elected in 1984 was committed to reforming and deregulating large parts of the New Zealand economy, including the broadcasting sector. In this context, the (political) scope for any growth in the licence fee was very limited and BCNZ was increasingly encouraged to operate as a commercial organisation. BCNZ's advertising volumes and revenues increased steadily throughout the 1980s – and dramatically so after deregulation in 1989.

The core objectives of the broadcasting sector reform process undertaken by the government were to increase sector investment and competition; to exploit the state-owned broadcaster as an income-generating asset; and to separate out 'social' objectives from commercial ones. These objectives underpinned the 1989 Broadcasting Act, which separated out the TV and radio businesses of BCNZ, leading to the creation of TVNZ – a 'state-owned enterprise' (SOE), to be run as a commercial business, focused on maximising its profits, which were to be returned as a dividend to the Treasury.

---

5   Source: New Zealand Broadcasters' Council, Sky Annual Reports, NZOA Annual Reports.

In addition, TVNZ would no longer receive directly the licence fee and, at the same time, its explicit responsibilities for delivering against the social purposes of broadcasting were dropped.[6] Instead, the Act transferred responsibility for collecting and distributing the public broadcasting licence fee to a new body – initially called the Broadcasting Commission, later changing its name to New Zealand On Air (NZOA). This reform established a 'contestable funding' model, under which any broadcaster or independent producer could bid for NZOA funding for programming that was deemed to serve PSB (social) purposes and which would not otherwise be commercially viable.[7] (The precise arrangements put in place for the contestable funding system are discussed in greater detail in the next section.)

Also in 1989, following two years of political negotiations, a third television channel, TV3, was launched. This was a commercial venture and was the first competitor to the TVNZ-owned channels, TV1 and TV2. TV3 is also able to apply to NZOA for public funding for particular programmes.

Throughout the 1990s, TVNZ was run as a commercial state asset, with the objective of maximising profits and with no explicit PSB remit; indeed, the National Party government, by then in power, was committed to privatising TVNZ and successive management teams were charged with preparing the company for sale. By the mid 1990s, TVNZ was amongst the world's most profitable broadcasting enterprises. Unsurprisingly, programmes intended to serve primarily 'social purposes' were only aired if they were funded by NZOA.

In 1999, in the run-up to parliamentary elections, the National Government also abolished the licence fee. While this might have seemed like a significant step, the consequences were limited. NZOA and PSB continued to be funded at the same level, but out of general taxation rather than an explicit licence fee.[8] The impact of the abolition of the licence fee on TVNZ was marginal, since it did not, in practice, affect its level of public funding or its relationship with NZOA or the government of the day. The key development for TVNZ had been the transfer of the receipt of the licence fee to NZOA, back in 1989.

Since the 1999 election (which Labour won), the political environment for PSB and TVNZ has changed once again. The new government was highly critical of

6   The key social purposes of broadcasting were defined as the provision of universal access for New Zealanders to a range of services that reflect and develop New Zealand's identity and culture.

7   NZOA is also responsible for funding two public radio stations, public music services, and other related areas, such as archiving activities. Funding for these services is allocated on a non-contested basis.

8   In 1999, NZOA's total funding was just under NZ$100 million (around £30 million).

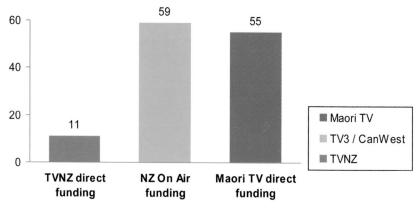

Figure 2. Public funding for PSB in New Zealand (NZ$ million, 2003).
[Source: TVNZ, Canwest, NZOA, TMP annual accounts.]

the strong commercial focus of TVNZ and rejected the options of an outright sale or part-privatisation. Instead, the government emphasised the public purposes of broadcasting and sought to re-focus TVNZ on those purposes. The 2003 TVNZ Act re-established TVNZ's 'CROC' status and its clear PSB remit.[9] TVNZ is now charged with fulfilling PSB purposes, as set out in its Charter, while at the same time 'maintaining its commercial performance'.

The current Labour government has raised the overall level of public funding for PSB (although it remains low, especially by international standards). For the first time since 1989, TVNZ has also recently been granted a small amount of direct funding (NZ$11 million in 2003, NZ$15 million in 2004), to support delivery against its new Charter and to supplement its own commercial revenues and the funding received from NZOA. Separately, a new PSB channel, 'Maori TV', has also been established, focused exclusively on reflecting and promoting the indigenous Maori language and culture. This channel receives direct public funding of NZ$55 million per year and is not entitled to apply for NZOA funding.

These new funding arrangements are summarised in the Figure 2.

The recent reforms of the New Zealand PSB sector under the current Labour government have not extended to NZOA, which remains largely as originally constituted. We now turn to a closer consideration of these arrangements.

---

9   See the 2003 TVNZ Act for TVNZ's Charter.

3. New Zealand's contestable funding model

NZOA's statutory arrangements and remit

NZOA is a Crown entity, wholly owned by the state, and funded out of general taxation revenues. Its responsibilities include the provision of funding for television, radio and a variety of music services. (As already mentioned, we only consider NZOA's television-related activities here.) Funding decisions are made by a Board of six Directors; each Director is appointed by the government of the day to serve terms of three years. These Directors are supported by twelve additional full-time staff, responsible for market analysis and general administrative duties.

NZOA's remit is clearly set out in the 1989 Broadcasting Act. In respect of television, it is required:

- 'to reflect and develop New Zealand identity and culture by promoting programmes about New Zealand interests [and] promoting Maori language and Maori culture';

- 'to ensure that a range of broadcasts is available to provide for the interests of women; children; the disabled; minorities';

- 'to ensure [... funding for...] drama and documentary programmes'.[10]

In addition, based on these purposes, NZOA sets annual strategic objectives and plans – both at a broad level and in relation to specific areas, such as drama or documentary programming.

The funding allocation process

The Board of Directors meets every two months to make funding decisions across all of its areas of responsibility. The number of funding applications considered at each meeting varies, with up to ten applications per meeting receiving a 'green light'.

Producers applying for NZOA funding must already have secured an agreement from a broadcaster that it will screen the programme, if funded. Moreover, NZOA will only ever provide part-funding for a programme – the remainder must come from the producer and/or broadcaster, as well as other funding bodies (e.g. the NZ Film Commission).

---

10   Broadcasting Act 1989.

Any application for NZOA funding must include:

- A programme or series synopsis
- A detailed description of the production team and schedule;
- A detailed budget, including the anticipated total cost of the production;
- An indication of the intended sources of funding for the production.[11]

Applications must be submitted one month in advance of NZOA's funding meetings; applicants are then usually contacted within three days of the meeting with a decision.

NZOA's appraisal of each application takes into account a range of criteria, but focuses on four areas in particular. First, does the proposed programme or series clearly serve NZOA's broad purposes and its specific strategic objectives, for that year? Historically, NZOA's funding decisions have reflected a clear focus on particular programming areas of priority, even though these areas can and do change over time.

Second, what is the proposed level of contribution (funding and/or resources) from other sources? Since NZOA never provides full funding for a project, this is vital – especially in the case of an application from an independent producer, when the level of support (whether funding or resources, such as studio time) from a broadcaster is seen as a key indicator of the likely eventual success of the project.

This leads on to the third main criterion: what is the likely audience size of the programme? This obviously depends upon the intended time slot for the programme, its genre, and the target audience ('mainstream' or niche). From early on, NZOA made clear that it was reluctant to fund programmes that would be watched by only a few (special interest) viewers. The first executive director of NZOA, Ruth Harley, declared that 'the challenge is not only to make programmes about New Zealanders and for New Zealanders, but to make programmes that they want to listen to or watch; programmes that appeal to a majority of our stakeholders'.

Finally, NZOA assesses the quality of the programme application itself: how strong, in creative and editorial terms, is the programme idea, the production team, the supporting research? This criterion has, arguably, not carried due

---

11 NZOA, Guidelines for television applications development funding.

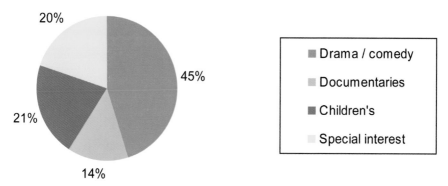

Figure 3. NZOA expenditure, by genre (NZ$ million, 2003).
[Source: NZOA 2003 Annual Report. 'Special interest' includes art, culture and performance.]

weight over the years, relative to the other considerations set out above – an argument to which we will return in the next section.

NZOA's interpretation of its remit

NZOA's funding is allocated across a range of programme genres, types, and formats – and also across different broadcasters and producers.

Genres and formats: NZOA has focused its funding on four core programming genres – drama (including comedy), documentaries, children's, and 'special' (minority) interest; it publishes an annual programming strategy for each of these areas. It very rarely funds sport or entertainment, which are considered to be commercially self-supporting, or news and current affairs – in part because this genre is also considered to be self-sustaining, but also because public funding for news can carry political sensitivities and risks. (TVNZ explicitly chooses not to use any of its direct public funding for its news output, for this reason.) NZOA's television funding split across genres has remained reasonably constant over time; Figure 3 gives the break-down in 2003.

NZOA has been willing to fund both one-off programmes and series, with each of these formats receiving, on average, a fairly equal share (i.e. 50 per cent each) of funding.

Local content: While the genre and format of a proposed programme are important, investment in programming made in New Zealand ('local content') is, and always has been, a top priority for NZOA. Its Directors have perceived local content as a vital means of 'reflecting and developing New Zealand identity and culture' – and have also placed great value on this programming achieving reach (in other words, being popular!).

This strategic focus in part reflects very particular market conditions in New Zealand: while in European or US markets, locally produced content accounts for the majority of terrestrial television schedules, in New Zealand, local content makes up only 20–25 per cent of the schedule. This situation is, in turn, a direct result of the respective costs of acquired and locally produced programming. Imported English language programming is very cheap for New Zealand broadcasters to acquire, both in absolute terms (New Zealand is often one of the last markets to which international distributors sell programme rights) and relative to locally produced content, which can cost anywhere between ten and twenty times more (on a per hour basis) than acquired programming.

In the highly commercial environment that has prevailed in the New Zealand PSB sector until recently, both the quantity and quality of 'local content' have therefore been at real risk, given the availability of cheaper, proven international 'hits'. NZOA has successfully targeted funding at local content production, as a matter of priority: since NZOA's inception, the total amount of local content has risen steadily, as has the share of peak-time that is locally produced.

Recipients of funding: Historically, most NZOA television funding goes directly to independent producers (85 per cent in 2003), with the remainder allocated to TVNZ in-house productions. This is primarily because the main terrestrial broadcasters (i.e. TVNZ and TV3) do not have in-house production teams in the genres which NZOA funds. (TVNZ and TV3 are essentially vertically separated broadcasters, with in-house production focusing on news and current affairs and other presenter-based genres, such as entertainment.) NZOA has also been keen to invest in the development of the New Zealand production sector and nurture a sustainable base of production capacity and skills.

The majority of the programmes receiving funding from NZOA are broadcast by TVNZ (80 per cent, compared to 20 per cent on TV3).

4. Evaluation of New Zealand's contestable funding model

New Zealand's contestable funding system remains in largely the same form as originally constituted, in spite of the extensive recent reform agenda of the current government. After fifteen years in operation, the system is seen by many as robust, effective in delivering specific PSB objectives and, overall, a success.

Contestable funding has delivered a number of significant benefits – notably, the promotion of transparency and efficiency of funding and the introduction of further competition into the PSB market. It has, however, been less successful in other respects – most significantly, in securing the effective and consistent delivery of high-quality PSB content with significant audience reach and impact. Its strengths and limitations reflect the fact that contestable funding is essentially a contract-based approach to PSB delivery, in which a publicly owned and funded body 'buys' or co-funds programming that serves specific (cultural / non-economic) purposes, that would not otherwise be provided by the market.

Strengths

The primary strengths of the contestable funding model are, first, that it has increased the regulatory accountability of public funding for PSB; and, second, that it has promoted competition and plurality in the supply of PSB. The New Zealand system has also proved itself capable of maintaining independence from both political and commercial interests.

Regulatory accountability: Contestable funding has improved the regulatory accountability of PSB delivery for three reasons. First, the system has ensured that public funding for programming is transparent. Any programme idea is assessed explicitly against PSB purposes before being granted funding and NZOA records exactly how much funding is allocated to which projects. This allows the 'output' (in the form of programmes and the impact of those programmes on audiences) to be clearly mapped and evaluated against the 'input' (the public funding).

Second, the system has allowed public funding to be channelled directly into the process of content creation – and has therefore helped to control the total public funding required for the provision of a given amount of PSB programming. NZOA has aimed to fund only the short-fall between the costs of production of a programme and the commercial (advertising) funding that would be generated by a programme. This 'top-up' approach has helped to avoid the public funding of programming that is likely to be commercially viable in its own right, or the funding of institutional overheads.

Third, NZOA has been able to target assistance at particular programme areas (in particular, local content) and audience groups (through minority programming) – and has been able to adjust or 'flex' its priorities on a year-by-year, or even programme-by-programme, basis. This has enabled NZOA to direct investment into those areas of PSB programming identified as most in need of support.

Competition and plurality: The independent production sector has been the primary beneficiary of the contestable funding system: it receives 85 per cent of NZOA funding and has grown significantly in scale since 1989. This larger and more stable domestic production base has, in turn, helped to improve programming diversity. Since the competitive funding process includes an assessment of the project budget and the scale of funding being requested in a project application, it has also helped to deliver PSB programming on a cost-effective basis.

The current funding system also gives independent producers some leverage over broadcasters when negotiating carriage and funding deals for PSB programming – since they have the option of switching to another broadcaster. This would not be the case if all public funding for PSB went to a single broadcaster, leaving producers beholden to that broadcaster.

There may be further value in the creative tension between funder and broadcaster: NZOA is better able to approach PSB delivery from a clear 'citizen' perspective, while TVNZ and TV3's 'consumer'–led perspective focuses more on potential audience size and reach. The advent of the long-running soap, *Shortland Street*, is often cited as a product of this creative tension: NZOA funding helped establish the programme and define its focus on New Zealand-specific issues, before it then grew into a commercial success which no longer required public funding.

While contestable funding has certainly promoted competition and plurality in the supply of PSB content, it has promoted only limited competition at channel level. The potential to apply for funding has helped to keep TV3 'at the PSB table', but only up to a point: TV3 broadcasts only 20 per cent of NZOA-funded productions and has not shown any real appetite for increasing its PSB output, as it has become increasingly focused on growing and defending its audience share in a fragmenting multi-channel market.

Independence from political and commercial interests: The New Zealand system has also demonstrated that a separate funding body can maintain its independence from both political and commercial interests. While many feared that NZOA would be a means by which the government would control the allocation of public funding for broadcasting, NZOA has been single-minded in defining its own priorities and pursuing them – often to the frustration of the Treasury. Equally, it has refused to submit to broadcaster pressure (especially from TVNZ) to promote or fund particular types of programming.[12] NZOA has established and promoted its own strategic and editorial objectives, even if, as a non-broadcasting body, it has not been in a position to deliver against objectives without buy-in from the broadcasters (as discussed in the following section).

---

12 For example, in 1989, TVNZ wanted NZOA to provide funding for a series of arts programmes. NZOA refused, as it was determined to provide funding only for programmes that would have broad appeal.

Limitations

The primary weakness of the New Zealand funding system is that it has not effectively and consistently, over time, delivered high quality, high impact PSB content. This is in large part because the system is predicated on a non-broadcaster body procuring delivery against a set of cultural and social objectives, that are not always easy to define, from a commercially focused and incentivised broadcast market. The NZOA funding application and negotiation process also represents an additional layer of regulatory activity and, at minimum, an additional set of administrative processes.

PSB quality and impact: The effectiveness of any PSB model must ultimately be judged in the light of the quality of PSB output and the impact of this output on audiences. Against these criteria, New Zealand's contestable funding model has been limited in its effectiveness.

The quality of PSB programming in New Zealand has suffered as a result of the funding system in place for three reasons. First, in the NZOA application process, the criterion of 'quality' has arguably been applied after that of programme origin and genre. NZOA has effectively prioritised local content over excellence or quality of programme-making.[13]

Second, applications for funding have often been 'thinned out', rather than trying to 'go the extra mile' in delivering a high-quality end product – because NZOA is perceived by producers as highly price-sensitive, as a result of its stated aim to provide funding only on a top-up basis.

Third, the requirement for independent producers to have broadcaster buy-in for a programme before being able to apply for NZOA funding is seen to have led to a narrowing in the types of programmes produced and an increase in the blandness of programming within specific PSB genres, most notably within documentaries and children's programming. Over time, producers have tended to make the types of programme that they know are most likely to be endorsed by the broadcasters (as the gatekeepers), ahead of NZOA's own preferences – in other words, those that follow a tried and tested formula and deliver reliable commercial performance.[14] The independent production sector, it would seem, has become driven more by the objective of securing funding than by programme innovation and creativity.

---

13 Over the past five years, no new NZ drama has, in critical terms, been perceived to be in the top ten dramas of the year.

14 For further analysis of this trend, see Paul Norris, *'Reshaping Public Broadcasting, the New Zealand Experience 1988 – 2003'* in *Public Service Communications*. ippr, 2004.

The impact on audiences of PSB content funded via the contestable funding system has also been limited. Despite NZOA's commitment to funding content with broad appeal, the moderate overall quality of NZOA-funded programming has failed to deliver high audience reach or appreciation. PSB output has also been fragmented across three different channels, in the form of individual programmes; this is a direct result of the nature of the contestable funding model, which effectively puts PSB delivery out to competitive tender on a product-by-product basis, rather than charging a dedicated broadcasting institution with ensuring effective PSB delivery, through deploying its wider schedule.

The 'gatekeeper' problem: NZOA has had considerable influence over New Zealand PSB, through its relationships with independent producers and broadcasters and through the funding it has made available for different programmes. Ultimately, however, it is reliant on the broadcasters themselves to agree to carry the programmes it is willing to fund. As a non-broadcasting body, NZOA is powerless to ensure that certain types of programmes get made or broadcast – especially if those programmes and the funding that NZOA can make available for them conflict with the broadcasters' focus on generating commercial revenues and returns.

Regulatory intervention: Although the contestable funding model was introduced as part of a raft of deregulatory measures, the establishment of a new regulatory body, in fact, increased the level of regulatory intervention in creative and editorial programme-making decisions. For example, NZOA has its own annual programming objectives and it, understandably, seeks to influence TVNZ's (and, to a lesser degree, TV3's) PSB programme strategy and funding.

This brings two major disadvantages. First, key creative and editorial decisions have been subject to approval by NZOA, rather than being the sole preserve of the broadcaster. Second, broadcasters' ability to plan their medium and longer-term programme strategies has been undermined, because there is a continual element of regulatory uncertainty over their future funding.

Additional administrative burden: Although NZOA is a very streamlined body (with fewer than 20 employees), it nevertheless constitutes an additional administrative burden on the core creative processes of content commissioning and production. For example, a producer with a particular idea for a documentary must first secure carriage and funding from a broadcaster for the programme, before then going through the NZOA funding application process. Final sign-off is often subject to negotiation and a range of specific conditions.

This dual process can inevitably slow down the 'green lighting' of a production and also increases programming costs, in the form of management time and transaction costs.[15]

Summary: a contract-based approach to PSB delivery

As a contractual arrangement, the contestable funding model has made the public funding process considerably more transparent, ensuring that the recipients of funding are explicitly accountable. It has also allowed public funding to be targeted at the specific areas judged to be in greatest need of public support. It has managed to do this with a relatively small budget and with apparently low levels of waste.

Contracts, however, rely on clear, up-front definition of terms and contestable funding has therefore, unsurprisingly, been most successful in securing the delivery of those aspects of PSB which can be specified. NZOA has been able to fund increases in hours of local content and of core PSB genres, including in peak-time. It has been unable, however, to specify or purchase the 'quality of service' of the contracted parties – the producers and the broadcasters – in their delivery of PSB, or their 'emotional' commitment to PSB purposes. Precisely because these most vital aspects of PSB are hard to define or measure, a contract-based approach, such as contestable funding, may struggle to promote – let alone guarantee – their effective delivery.

5. Lessons for the UK

The UK and New Zealand broadcasting markets differ in many respects, and any lessons from the New Zealand funding experience must be drawn with appropriate care. Yet it seems safe to conclude that certain core strengths and limitations of a contestable funding system would also apply in the UK. Aspects of the above analysis may therefore usefully inform the current public policy debate about future funding arrangements for PSB – in particular, with regard to whether, and in what circumstances, contracts may be used effectively as a means of delivering certain aspects of PSB, potentially in harness with existing PSB institutions.

Market differences

Most obviously, the UK market is far larger than New Zealand's, with 60 million viewers and 25 million homes, compared to 4 million viewers and 1.4 million

---

15 Interviews with TVNZ programming executives.

homes. In 2003, UK TV revenues were around £10 billion, compared to just under UK£400 million in New Zealand.

More significantly, the scale and structure of PSB provision in the two countries is very different: annual public funding for PSB (TV and radio) in the UK is in the region of US$6 billion, compared to US$100 million in New Zealand. The UK has four established public service broadcasters (the BBC, ITV, Channel 4, and Five) with clearly defined PSB remits and obligations, two of which (the BBC and Channel 4) are not-for-profit, with the BBC's public services almost wholly publicly funded, via the licence fee. In New Zealand, TVNZ is the only broadcaster with a PSB remit, and both it and TV3 remain primarily commercially funded.

So, the UK has a 'cornerstone' public service broadcaster, in the form of the BBC, along with a range of further well established broadcasters with PSB remits, in a way that is simply not the case in New Zealand. These market differences mean that, if a contestable funding system were to be introduced in the UK, it would operate in radically different conditions – and might therefore have some different strengths and limitations.

Finally, while there is some overlap in the broad PSB purposes in each country, most notably in the areas of reflecting and promoting national cultures and identities, specific objectives and priorities in each country differ significantly. For example, as already discussed, one of the key regulatory objectives in New Zealand has been to increase significantly the levels of locally produced content, given the relative economics of local, versus internationally acquired, programming. Locally produced programming is also a key regulatory objective in the UK, but is seen as a necessary, but not a sufficient, condition of PSB delivery: while local production is easily specified, the successful delivery of PSB must meet a complex series of purposes and characteristics (as recently described by Ofcom).

Lessons from New Zealand for the UK

Notwithstanding these differences, the experience of New Zealand's contestable funding system might, at a general level, offer some lessons for the UK.

On the plus side, introducing a contestable funding model to the UK could bring a higher level of transparency to public funding for PSB – certainly if it replaced the current implicit subsidies (such as discounted analogue spectrum prices) in the system, which are not clearly defined either in their value or in their allocation between different programming areas. Contestable funding could also provide greater regulatory flexibility – whether via Ofcom or a new intermediary funding body or 'Arts Council of the Air' – over the allocation of funding, between different programming types or genres, or between services targeted at specific social groups.

It is somewhat less clear whether contestable funding would effectively promote further competition and plurality in the UK system. At the level of PSB supply, the UK already has a vibrant and pluralistic independent production sector – which can be seen as already providing a form of contestable funding, via the BBC's and ITV's independent production quotas. The recent changes in the terms of trade between broadcasters and producers should help to re-inforce the strength of the independent sector.

At the level of competition between public service broadcasters, could contestable funding be a means of enabling ITV, Channel 4 and Five, to continue to supply certain key PSB services, even as the commercial case for their doing so diminishes, as we move towards digital switch-over? Certainly, it is one potential means of allocating public money to these broadcasters. It is unclear, however, whether such an approach would be the most effective means of funding (non-BBC) PSB provision.[16]

In the case of Channel 4, inserting an intermediary funding body, with its own distinct decision-making processes, could (seriously) undermine the broadcaster's editorial independence and its ability to deliver 'innovation, experiment and creativity',[17] which lie at the heart of its remit and PSB 'value'. The New Zealand model has certainly struggled to deliver the key 'characteristics' of PSB, such as innovation and originality; in fact it has had a narrowing effect (as described in section 4) on programme-making in key PSB genres, including documentaries and children's. Furthermore, contestable funding would be unlikely to provide the secure and stable longer term funding required to support the kind of risk-taking which volatile commercial markets are unlikely to deliver.

Contestable funding might be a means of keeping ITV and Channel 5 'at the PSB table' – but it is hardly compatible with a light-touch regulatory approach, given the additional levels of administration involved in such a system. It would also risk the same gatekeeper issues, described above, that the New Zealand system has experienced, as well as the likely misalignment between, on the one hand,

---

16 We have not considered the viability of contestable funding for the BBC here, since it has not been considered by Ofcom as a serious policy option or replacement mechanism for the licence fee.
17 Communications Act 2003, s265 [3].

the social or cultural purposes of public policy and, on the other, the commercial objectives of ITV and Five.

Contracts versus institutions

Given the concerns expressed above, is the contestable funding model of no clear use to UK PSB? The UK system is currently based around strong PSB institutions, rather than clearly specified contracts – with the BBC as the cornerstone and ITV, Channel 4 and Five playing complementary roles. The long-term stability of the historical PSB compact has allowed these broadcasters to develop institutional skills and cultures well suited to PSB delivery.

The strength of both the BBC and Channel 4 as vehicles for PSB delivery derives from and rests upon both their core institutional purposes and their not-for-profit status. It is difficult to imagine satisfactorily replacing these arrangements with a contractual approach to delivery. ITV, on the other hand, is somewhat different: historically, it has been a vital PSB provider, while also operating as a privately owned, profit-making business. In effect, ITV has had a contract with its regulator: in return for privileged (and discounted) access to analogue spectrum, ITV has undertaken to deliver specific types and levels of PSB programming, from national and regional news to religious and arts programming.

Ofcom has concluded that the current compact is not sustainable, leading up to and beyond digital switch-over, and that, from a commercial point of view, ITV's PSB commitments are unlikely to remain viable.[18] Depending upon Ofcom's eventual PSB priorities, a form of contestable funding could be used to procure, via a competitive process, some of the elements of PSB provision that may be given up by ITV – especially those that can be sufficiently clearly specified in a contract with a third party provider (either ITV itself or alternative providers).[19] In this respect, a contractual approach to the procurement and funding of specific, clearly defined areas of PSB could complement and strengthen the core UK institutional PSB system.

In light of the lessons from the New Zealand model, however, it is far more questionable whether contestability could, on a broader scale, replace existing institutions in the delivery of PSB. Given the inherent difficulty in defining

18 Ofcom *PSTB Review Phase 2 Report*, September 2004.

19 For example, if Ofcom wants to sustain plurality of regional and local news provision, over and above the BBC's services, it could, perhaps, contract out this area of PSB provision, based on explicit and transparent terms, in the same way that Channel 4 has successfully contracted out its news service to ITN.

particular aspects of the prescribed purposes and characteristics of UK PSB, these institutions, and the experience, skill sets and ethos they have built up over an extended period of time, seem better equipped to meet the challenge of 'maintaining and strengthening the quality of public service television broadcasting in the United Kingdom'.[20]

20 Communications Act 2003, s264(3).

Notes on the Contributors

Dieter Helm is an economist, specialising in utilities, infrastructure, regulation and the environment, and concentrates on the energy, water, communications and transport sectors in Britain and Europe. He is currently a Fellow in Economics, New College, Oxford. He holds a number of advisory board appointments, including the Prime Minister's Council for Science and Technology, the Defra Academic Panel (Chair), the DTI Sustainable Energy Panel Advisory Board, and the Ministerial Task Force on Sustainable Development. He is a director of OXERA Holdings Ltd and Helm Associates Ltd, providing consulting services to chairmen and chief executives of leading utilities and financial companies.

Damian Green has been Member of Parliament for Ashford since 1997. He has been Shadow Education Secretary and Shadow Transport Secretary, and has also been a Conservative Spokesman on Employment and the Environment. He served on the Culture, Media and Sport Select Committee from 1997–98.
He previously worked in the Prime Minister's Policy Unit from 1992–94, advising on media policy. He has also been Policy Director of the European Media Forum, and written a number of publications on Broadcasting Policy. He is a former financial journalist, working for the BBC, ITN, and Business Television.

Mark Oliver is Managing Director of Oliver & Ohlbaum Associates Limited (O&O). He founded O&O in 1995, and has since advised a number of leading media, entertainment and sports organisations on strategy and finance. He was an adviser to the UK Government on the Communications White Paper in 2000, advised the Number 10 Policy Unit on aspects of the Communications Bill and is currently a member of the DCMS's Media Experts Panel. From 1989 to 1995, he was Head of Strategy at the BBC, advising the Board on all strategic and financial issues.

Simon Terrington co-founded Human Capital, the media and research consultancy, in 1995. Since then he has advised clients in television, radio, magazines, newspapers and online media on strategy, research and creative development. Simon also works on research into social choice theory at London University.

Caroline Dollar has worked at Human Capital for two years, specialising in research and development. Before working at Human Capital she was a strategic planner at Trinity Mirror. She has a degree in modern languages from Cambridge University.

Andrew Graham is the Master of Balliol College, Oxford, a non-Executive Director of Channel 4 Television, Chairman of the Advisory Board of the Oxford Internet Institute (which he played the lead in creating) and a Trustee of the Esmee Fairbairn Foundation. He advised the Prime Minister, 1967–69 and 1974–76; and, from 1988–94, the Leader of the Labour Party, John Smith. He wrote (with Gavyn Davies) *Broadcasting, Society and Policy in the Multimedia Age*, now part of the standard defence of public service broadcasting.

Bill Robinson is the Head UK Business Economist at PricewaterhouseCoopers (PwC) LLP. He has been a Special Adviser to the Chancellor of the Exchequer, Director of the Institute for Fiscal Studies, a Director of London Economics, and head of macro-economic forecasting at the London Business School. He has worked on a range of projects for media clients, including the BBC, and was a member of the expert panel on the ITC Programme Supply Review. Bill has a particular interest in funding issues, and has recently completed a major project for Ofcom looking at the future of advertising revenues.

John Raven is an Assistant Director in the PwC Economics Team. He specialises in quantitative analytical and modelling techniques to find solutions for organisations in the entertainment, leisure and media sectors. John has gained seven years experience in this field after completing his masters in economics at the London School of Economics.

Lit Ping Low joined PwC Economics as a consultant in 2003 after graduating from the University of Cambridge. She focuses on the media sector, helping clients with analytical economics and quantitative economics.

Gavyn Davies (OBE) is Chairman of Fulcrum Asset Management. He was Chairman of the BBC from October 2001 until he resigned after the Hutton Inquiry Report on 28 January 2004. Before that, he was Vice Chairman of the BBC, and in 1999 he chaired a UK Government inquiry into the Future Funding of the BBC. He was an economic adviser to the 10 Downing Street Policy Unit

(1976–79); an economist with Phillips and Drew (1979–81); Chief Economist, Simon & Coates (1981–86) and Head of Global Economics and Chairman of Investment Research at Goldman Sachs (1986–2001). From 1992–97, he was a member of HM Treasury's independent forecasting panel and has been Visiting Professor at the London School of Economics and an economic adviser to the House of Commons Treasury Select Committee.

Jeremy Mayhew is a Partner at Spectrum Strategy Consultants, where he heads the Media Regulation and Public Service Broadcasting Practice. His recent work has included projects for broadcasters, telecos, regulators and the Graf Independent Review of BBC Online. He is also a Non-Executive Member of the Strategic Rail Authority Board. Previously, Jeremy has been BBC Worldwide's Director of New Media (1995–1999) and Director of New Ventures and Strategy (1999–2001); the BBC's Head of Strategy Development (1993–95); and Special Adviser at the Department of Trade and Industry (1990–92) and at the Department of Social Security (1992–93).

Luke Bradley-Jones is a manager at Spectrum Strategy Consultants and focuses on regulation, public policy and new business development in the broadcasting and new media sectors. He has worked for the UK Government, regulators in the UK and Brazil, broadcasters, and fixed and mobile operators. Recent projects include providing advisory support to the Graf review of BBC Online and for TV New Zealand, developing a PSB and commercial performance reporting framework.